The Use of the Bible
in Preaching

REGINALD H. FULLER

The Use of the Bible
in Preaching

THE BIBLE READING FELLOWSHIP

To Donald Coggan
101st Archbishop of Canterbury
who by teaching and example
has shown what
biblical preaching
should be

First published 1981

© REGINALD H. FULLER 1981

BRF Book Club no. 9

Printed in the United States of America

British Library CIP Data

Fuller, Reginald Horace
  The use of the Bible in preaching.
  1. Bible—Homiletical use   2.   Preaching
  I.   Title.
  251   BV4211.2
  ISBN 0–900164–54–9

The Bible Reading Fellowship

BRF encourages regular, informed Bible-reading as a means of renewal in the churches. BRF publishes daily readings, with explanatory notes; group study material; paperback books; audio-visual aids, etc.

BRF : St Michael's House, 2 Elizabeth Street, London SW1

BRF : P.O. Box M, Winter Park, Florida 32790

BRF : Room 305, Woden Churches Centre, Philip ACT 2606, Australia

Contents

1

Has the Bible Lost
Its Authority?

"The Word of the Lord"—"Thanks be to God." This way of
concluding Scripture readings has been introduced into our churches
quite recently. People react to it in different ways. Some like
it, because they understand the Bible to be literally the Word of
God, fallen down from heaven, verbally inspired, inerrant, and in-
fallible. Every statement, even in some cases the account of creation
in Genesis (sometimes including the date 4004), is accepted (at
least in America) as revealed truth.[1] Such people we usually call
fundamentalists.

There are others who don't like saying "The Word of the Lord"
at the end of Scripture readings, precisely because they think it
means what the fundamentalists mean by it, and they find such a
position untenable in the modern world. The most extreme version
of this view is that propounded by Dennis Nineham,[2] a view which
also finds expression in the Church of England doctrinal report
called *Christian Believing*.[3] For those who think this way, the Bible
is mostly old hat. It is the way people talked about their religious
experiences centuries ago—actually spread over more than a millen-
nium, so we should rather speak of "ways," in the plural. And for
us in the twentieth century, their ways cannot be our ways. For we
live in a world whose thinking has been irrevocably shaped by
factors and forces our forefathers knew nothing about—by Darwin,
Marx, Freud, Einstein. The Bible is for good or ill culturally conditioned. Part of this cultural conditioning is the exclusive claim it
makes for the biblical revelation. That goes both for the Old Testament and for the New. In the Old, Israel claims a monopoly of the
truth: "Thou shalt have no other gods but me." Only in Jerusalem,
where God has chosen to put his name, is the place where true

worship is offered. And in the New Testament the Apostle Peter claims that there is no other name under heaven and on earth by which we must be saved but by Christ alone (see Acts 4:12). And that "alone" is powerfully enforced by Paul in his message of justification by grace through faith. Such exclusive claims are felt to be untenable in an age where first imperial expansion, then modern transport and two-way immigration have made us familiar with the great religions of the East, held and practiced perhaps by the people living next door—especially if we happen to live in Southall or Notting Hill, in New York City or Washington, D.C. Pluralism, cultural relativity, exclusiveness—these then are three features of the Bible which cause even holders of church-related positions in Oxford or Cambridge, or in the "departments of religion" in secular American universities, to question the authority of the Bible.

Both of these attitudes to the Bible, the fundamentalist and the radical, have their consequences for the use or nonuse of the Bible in preaching. Fundamentalists are likely to go on repeating what "the Bible says"—making no effort to translate it into a living message for today. For them, too, it becomes just as important (sometimes it seems even more important) to insist that Jonah was swallowed by a whale (or, for some reason I cannot comprehend, they are particularly insistent that it was a "great fish"—as though that really made any difference!), as that God was in Christ reconciling the world to himself.

Small wonder that on the other hand the radicals tell preachers to throw their Bibles away, to read the *London Times* in Britain (in the days before the strike closed it down) or the *New York Times* in the United States, pray about it, and study the mystics. This is no caricature, for I have heard Dennis Nineham say just that.

No doubt the present writer, Anglican as he is, is constitutionally disposed to look for the middle way. But in this case he is profoundly convinced that the middle way happens to be right. For there is truth in the fundamentalist position and there is truth in the radical. One of the chief criticisms to be brought against James Barr's devastating attack on fundamentalism in his book of that title is that he won't allow them to be right about anything at all.[4] What then are the things the fundamentalists are right about? Two points in the main.

First, we must affirm that in the Bible we hear more than just the speech of human beings. "Thus saith the Lord," the prophets proclaim again and again. Peter and Paul have a holy constraint from outside laid upon them: "Woe is me if I preach not the gospel." They are not just saying what they want to say; indeed, sometimes they feel forced to say what they would rather not say. There is, then, a superhuman quality to the Bible, and that is why the Christian church has always called it *also*, as well as a human product (which it undoubtedly is as we see from Luke 1:1–4), the Word of God. For the Christian church to abandon that affirmation would be for it to lose its very identity.

Secondly, the fundamentalists often make the scholarly critics cringe by the way they treat the Old Testament as direct data for Christian faith—as though God were announcing Christian doctrine through Moses and the prophets and as though the human authors were fully conscious of this and intended it. The headings at the top of the page and at the head of the chapters in the Authorized (King James) Version encourage this approach. To take one page at random, Isaiah 49 is headed: "Christ, being sent to the Jews, complaineth of them: he is sent to the Gentiles. God's love to the church perpetual." (It needs hardly be said that these headings are not part of Scripture but were compiled by the translators.) Yet the fundamentalists, however wrong, do have a point. This is, the essential unity between the Old Testament and New within the perspective of Christian faith. It is the same God who discloses himself in both the Old Testament and the New—and that despite all the varieties of time, circumstance, and the persons of the human writers. We shall come back to this point later.

But there are reasons why we cannot accept the fundamentalist position. The primary one is our own intellectual integrity. God has given us brains to use, and with their brains European (mostly German) scholars have evolved the historical-critical method. Insofar as the Bible is the product of human history, we can't just leave our brains—our historical-critical brains—outside when we come to study the Bible. Here we are different from our forebears, and here we have to agree with the radicals like Dennis Nineham and his ilk. We cannot read Genesis 1 and 2 as though Galileo, Darwin, and Einstein had never existed. If we hear the Word of God in these chapters it does not come to us as information—not even as revealed information—about *how* the world came into being. It comes to us as *proclamation*, announcing to us through the medium of now-antiquated mythology the message that God is the source and ground of all being. Here we have to distinguish between the medium and the message.

The doctrine of verbal inspiration breaks down, too, because of the countless textual variations in the early manuscripts of the Old and New Testaments on which we depend for our knowledge of what the authors wrote. Which text, then, would be verbally inspired? We know now that the so-called Textus Receptus ("Received Text"), a type of text on which the Luther Bible and the AV (KJV) were based, is a later standardized text, certainly not as close as we can get today to the originals. We know for instance that the so-called Johannine comma, 1 John 5:7, is not part of the original text, and is not therefore a divine revelation of the doctrine of the Trinity. (This writer believes, of course, the doctrine of the Trinity, but not on the strength of that spurious text.) So we are left asking, if the Bible is verbally inspired, which text is it? The Textus Receptus and the AV (KJV)? Or if not, the original autographs? But these we can never recover, however much we do our best to get back to the earliest text possible.

Then thirdly, there is historical criticism. There are contradictions of fact between the synoptic Gospels and the Fourth Gospel. Jesus cleanses the temple at the end of his ministry—just before the passion—in the synoptists (that is, Matthew, Mark, and Luke), and almost at the beginning of it in John. They cannot both be right, and the old solution that he did it twice is discredited as illegitimate harmonization. According to Luke, Jesus was born at the time of the census in Judea. We know from external sources that that census took place in A.D. 6 and was understandably organized after the deposition of Archelaus and the incorporation of Judea into the Roman Empire. Yet Matthew—and indeed Luke elsewhere by implication—places the birth of Jesus before the death of Herod the Great, that is, 4 B.C. or a little earlier. Valiant efforts to argue for an earlier census are only unconvincing attempts to save the historical veracity of Luke.

No, there is only one possible conclusion. Although Christian faith (including that of the fundamentalists) may legitimately find in the Bible the Word of God, that Word is subject to the fallibility of the human authors who wrote it. What that Word is, and how it is present even in the fallible words of the human authors, we shall discuss later.

We turn now to the radicals. One of the most remarkable features of the report *Christian Believing* is the basic conception of faith with which it was operating. For it seemed to think of faith almost exclusively in terms of a list of theological tenets proposed for individual acceptance. It discussed those which in the view of the authors, or some of them, were difficult for modern people to accept, and then proceeded to strip down the rest to a minimum the individual believer could get away with and still be a Christian. Despite the presence of some evangelicals, even conservative evangelicals, on the doctrinal commission, the terms in which the whole investigation was conducted were distinctly unevangelical. For what the Bible proposes to us for our faith is not a washing bill of items to be believed or about which one has difficulties, but a proclamation, a message of what God has done for us. When a friend has done something for you, you do not analyze what he/she has done, then discuss what you can accept and what you can't. You gratefully acknowledge and accept the gift, and respond to the giver with the whole of your person. That is the kind of faith the Bible calls from us. For the Bible contains the message of what God has done for us and for our salvation. And it invites the total response of our person. Of course that includes our brains, too. But we have to use them, not to analyze what has been done and chop it up into bits and pieces, some of which we accept and others we throw away. We have to use our brains to comprehend what is the height and depth and length and breadth of what God has done for us. The authors of *Christian Believing* were using their brains altogether in the wrong way.

What then of their specific points of objection to the biblical message? First, there is their concern about cultural conditionedness. This of course is no new discovery. It has been known ever since the Babylonian creation epic was discovered, and the degree of dependence of the Genesis creation story upon it. It has been known ever since we became aware that Jesus' message of the Kingdom was couched in terms of Jewish apocalyptic, the message of the earliest post-Easter community in terms both of apocalyptic and of Jewish nationalist messianism, and the message of Greek-speaking Christianity in terms borrowed from the mystery religions and the early stages of what later became Gnosticism. But these things do not affect the message itself. Genesis still proclaims God as our Creator, the source and ground of all that is. Jesus still confronts us with the immediate, saving presence of God. The preaching of the early church still addresses us with a message of salvation, inaugurated in the Jesus event, constantly made present in Word and Sacrament and with a sense of present incompleteness pointing forward and crying out for future consummation. All of this is expressed in culturally conditioned language. But the encounter with Jesus is mediated through that language, and that is what matters.

Secondly, there is the radical charge that the Bible is so pluralistic that it is impossible to distill from it any consistent beliefs about anything. Fashions in this matter are constantly changing. Earlier in this century, scholars were writing books with such titles as ''The Varieties of New Testament Religion.'' Then in the forties and fifties they were writing books with such titles as ''The Unity of the New Testament,'' finding that unity in the ''kerygma,'' or message. Now it is fashionable to emphasize the ''pluralism'' of the Bible once more. We are told that the New Testament has *kerygmata* (plural, ''messages'') rather than *a* kerygma. What is the truth here? Surely, as usual, there is truth on both sides. A more balanced view will be found in a book like James D. G. Dunn's *Unity and Diversity in the New Testament*,[5] which seeks to establish a consistent and unifying strand and an integrating center for the diverse expressions of New Testament Christianity. So, as is so often the case, the radicals are partly right and partly wrong.

The third charge the radicals bring against the Bible is its exclusiveness. They are prepared to say that for us as Christians Jesus Christ as presented by the Bible is the ultimate and final disclosure of God. But only for us as Christians. For people of other traditions, their religions are just as valid. Now this ignores what in technical language we call the ''eschatological'' nature of the Christ event. By this we mean that the end and goal of history has already happened in advance and in principle in the life, death, and resurrection of Jesus Christ. This claim of finality is absolutely integral to the core of Jesus' message of the Kingdom of God. It belongs to the very nature of his word and work. You cannot say that you will accept his word and work, but not the finality of it: for then you are accepting something else. And this Christ event is something that has happened. It is not just a set of human ideas or notions. Really there is no such thing as "Christianity" in the Bible (you won't find the word in a concordance). There is the proclamation of an event that happened. You can accept it or reject it, but you cannot cause it not to have happened.

To insist on the exclusiveness and finality of the Christ event does not compel us to take a completely negative attitude to other religions. The prologue to St. John's Gospel helps us here. It speaks of the Logos (that is, God in the act of self-communication) as the light that enlightens every man. We can accept all that is true in other religions as the consequence of this "general revelation." We can extend what the author of the Letter to the Hebrews wrote in respect of the Old Testament to cover the other religions outside of the Bible: "In many and various ways God spoke of old to our fathers by the prophets; but in these last days he has spoken to us by a Son" (Heb. 1:1 RSV). Such insights provide the basis for a positive yet qualified evaluation of human religions. They include (along with error) valid insights into God, the world, and humanity which Christian faith can affirm to be the result of the work of the Logos, to use St. John's language, or of that partial and fragmentary speaking, as the author of Hebrews phrases it.

But these disclosures of God are precisely partial and fragmentary. Only in the Christ event is there complete disclosure. Only in him does the fullness of the Godhead dwell bodily. Only in him has God acted for our salvation once for all. Only if what we are basically concerned with is a human thing, Christianity, a set of human notions about God, the world, and humanity, could we legitimately debate the finality of that thing as the radicals do. But since we are concerned with an event, the final verdict on all human religions is that none of them proclaim that event. Only the Bible and the church with the Bible in its hand can do that.

The proclamation of an event—it is that proclamation that we call the Word of God. It is that proclamation that we find in the Bible, in the Old Testament and in the New. Now of course we do not find that proclamation in the same way in the Old Testament as we find it in the New. We do not have to subscribe to such a statement as that we have already quoted from the Authorized (King James) Version, namely that in Isaiah "Christ, being sent to the Jews, complaineth of them." Rather, in the Old Testament we find the Word who is (later) to become incarnate (*Logos incarnandus*), whereas in the New Testament we find the Word who has become incarnate (*Logos incarnatus*). The Word that is to become incarnate is always fragmentary and various. The partial, fragmentary Word of the Old Testament is spoken in two basic ways, in promise and in type. Let us consider each in turn.

First, promise. When we promise to do something for a friend, we often do not know precisely how we shall do it. Later circumstances will have to determine that. But we give him our word that somehow or other we will be there to help him. We shall see him through, and we ask him to take us at our word. The Old Testament promises are something like that. God does not predict precisely what he will do when he comes finally for our salvation. He does so in various and fragmentary ways. From Isaiah 53 we catch some glimpse that that mode of his action will involve vicarious suffering. Yet from Psalm 2 we should gather rather that it would involve a military victory. We can now of course put all the pieces together. But before Christ came that would not have been possible. That is why the messianic expectations of Israel took so many different forms.

In dealing with these promises we must be careful not to deny the integrity of God's history with Israel. When Isaiah 53 was first promulgated, it had to do with the history of Israel in exile and its return from Babylon. That was the original application of the text. But texts live on. They enshrine certain valid insights into God's dealing with his people that will recur. And every act of Yahweh contains a promise of greater things to follow.[6] So when those greater things do follow, fresh meaning lights upon the text. We can now read Isaiah 53 on Good Friday and hear in it the passion of our Lord, not because the prophet was consciously predicting it, nor because that was Yahweh's intended message to Israel at the time, but because we can now for the first time see in it a promise which has finally come to rest in the Christ event.

As well as the promise of God, there are also recurring patterns of

God's action. Already the Old Testament writers were aware of this. The unknown prophet of the Exile once again presents the return from exile as a reliving of the Exodus:

In the wilderness prepare the way of the Lord,
make straight in the desert a highway for our God.
Every valley shall be lifted up,
and every mountain and hill be made low;
the uneven ground shall become level,
and the rough places a plain.

(Isa. 40:3–4 RSV)

It is not that history repeats itself. It is that God is consistent in himself. When he acts he does the same sort of things, and therefore his actions have a consistent pattern. Thus in Exodus Yahweh says that he has heard of the sufferings of his people and promises that he will "come down" and deliver them (Exod. 3:8). That is a remarkable word. Of course, our radicals will quibble about it. It implies a pre-Copernican universe. Maybe. But there is more to it than that. When God acts it is an act of *condescension*, of self-humiliation from his exalted state. As the Germans would put it, *Er lässt sich herab*, literally "He lets himself down." The pattern of condescension comes out again in the Christ event:

though he was in the form of God,
did not count equality with God a thing to be grasped,
but emptied himself,
taking the form of a servant.

(Phil. 2:6–7 RSV)

And the Nicene Creed picks up the biblical language of condescension when it says, "who for us men and for our salvation came down from heaven."

The Exodus also gives us the pattern of transition. Israel passes from slavery to freedom, from darkness to light, from death to life. And so the Exodus became the supreme model for the Easter event.

Again, the Old Testament provides us with the language of vindication. It is the pattern of God's dealing with his people that he steps in and vindicates his servants when they are at the end of their tether. This pattern especially shapes the psalms, as for instance Psalms 22 and 69. The present writer experienced this pattern in the Psalter as a chorister in a Church of England parish, where the psalms were sung to Anglican chant. So often, as in Psalm 22, sung as it was in the double chant by Matthew Camidge, the first half would be in the minor key, and then at verse 22 it would shift triumphantly to the major. That taught me what the pre-Pauline formula in 1 Cor. 15:3–4 meant when it said that "Christ died for our sins in accordance with the scriptures . . . he was raised . . . in accordance with the scriptures" (RSV). Consistency of pattern in God's acts, finding their culmination in the Christ event—that is what we find in the Bible, Old Testament and New. It is in *this* sense that the Old Testament speaks of Christ and that we can find the gospel there. It is in this sense that as Article VII of the Thirty-nine Articles has it, "The Old Testament is not contrary to the New: for both in the Old and New Testament everlasting life is offered to Mankind by Christ."

How then are we to reconcile the presence of the Word of God in the Bible with a recognition of its human qualities, its error, fallibility, cultural relativity, and the like? The answer is that these human qualities belong to the earthly vessels in which the heavenly treasure is contained. We have here once more a pattern of God's action which runs all through his way with us. Not only is his Word given through human words; his Sacraments show precisely the same pattern. Bread and wine, weak, beggarly elements though they be, truly convey the body and blood of Christ after a heavenly and spiritual manner to the faithful receiver. The church of Jesus Christ, his body, is known to us only in the guise of a frail, sin-laden human institution. And it is the pattern of the incarnation itself: in Jesus Christ that aspect of the being of God which is himself going forth in self-communication became a finite human being, with all the limitations (save, we believe, sin) of a first-century Palestinian Jew. If we have this heavenly treasure which we call the Bible in earthly vessels, then the fundamentalists deny the earthliness of the vessel (which is parallel to monophysitism in Christology or transubstantiation in sacramental doctrine). The radicals on the other hand deny the heavenly treasure (which is like those Christologies which deny the divinity of Christ, and that low doctrine of the Sacraments which sees the elements only as bare signs).

If Scripture is the Word of God insofar as it proclaims to us Christ (*was Christum treibet*, as Luther said), this means that it, the witness of the prophets and apostles to the Christ event, is the Word of God only within the believing community. Only there does the Word *happen* as Word. Shut up in a book, the Word is silent. The Bible is Word only as it is proclaimed Word. How then shall they hear without a preacher?

This is where the preacher comes into the picture. Preaching is not just an optional activity we do with the Bible. It is absolutely integral to the Bible as Word. Or, to pick up the image we used above, preachers are necessary to uncover the treasure that is in the earthly vessel. They have the task of identifying and exposing that treasure in each pericope (unit) of Scripture. To do this they require two major aids: first there is the technique of exegesis (which we shall discuss in the next chapter), and then the aid of the tradition of the believing community (which we shall discuss in chapter 3).

NOTES

1. Properly speaking, what we call "fundamentalism" is more aptly designated "Reformed scholasticism." As a self-conscious reaction to biblical criticism it originated in Princeton—its founders were Charles Hodge and B. B. Warfield—whence it spread throughout English-speaking Protestantism in the mid to late nineteenth century.

2. Dennis E. Nineham, *The Use and Abuse of the Bible* (London: Macmillan & Co.; New York: Barnes & Noble, 1976).

3. Archbishops' Commission on Christian Doctrine, *Christian Believing* (London, 1976).

4. James Barr, *Fundamentalism* (Philadelphia: Westminster Press, 1978).

5. James D. G. Dunn, *Unity and Diversity in the New Testament* (Philadelphia: Westminster Press, 1977).

6. This has been brought very powerfully in the theology of hope. See especially Jürgen Moltmann, *Theology of Hope* (New York: Harper & Row, Publishers, 1976).

2
Exegesis:
What and How?

There is a good deal of confusion in the theological world as to precisely what exegesis is. There are those (notably Bultmann and his followers) who hold that exegesis involves establishing what the text *means* so that it speaks to us today. There are others (notably Krister Stendahl in his celebrated article "Biblical Theology" in the *Interpreter's Dictionary of the Bible*) who maintain that exegesis is concerned to establish what the text *meant* originally. There is something to be said in favor of both views. On the one hand, to be concerned with what the text *means* is to prevent our use of the Bible from becoming merely a dry-as-dust historical enterprise, something purely academic and antiquarian. It is a necessary challenge to the way the Bible is being studied in the departments of religion in modern secular universities.[1] Studied simply in terms of what it meant, the Bible would be a fit addition to the bibliography of classical studies, along with Homer and Herodotus, Vergil and Livy. Even if one argues with the existentialist that such study is not just a detached and disinterested study of the past, since all study of the human past discloses possibilities for the understanding of human existence today, that is not enough. Our concern as Christians with the Bible is not that it merely exposes possible understandings of human existence, but that it discloses to us the Word of God, that it preaches to us Christ for our salvation.

Indeed, Bultmann himself contributed to that modern, secular, humanistic understanding of the study of the Bible because he believed the only way the Bible could be made to speak today was precisely as disclosing possibilities of human self-understanding (the so-called existential interpretation). As one reads Bultmann's exegetical work, one feels all too often that he modernizes the biblical material by forcing it into the categories of German existentialist philosophy. Just one example. Bultmann maintains that the real meaning of the statement that "God raised Jesus from the dead" is that the preaching of the cross today offers us the possibility of entering into what he calls authentic existence. All that is true as far as it goes, but it is confusing cause with effect and misinterpreting the message of the New Testament. When the New Testament writers proclaimed that God had raised Jesus from the dead they meant that God had done something to Jesus—taken him out of his past and made him our living Lord. And it is as living Lord that he offers us—if you like to use Bultmann's terms—the possibility of authentic existence. It seems therefore that if we follow Bultmann's concept of exegesis we shall end up with eisegesis—reading *into* the text our own ideas. Against that we need a much more objective control. This brings us back to Krister Stendahl's conception of exegesis— that it is concerned to establish what the text *meant*. I believe this is right. But we can only avoid making this a purely academic exercise if we see exegesis as a first step toward something else, if we understand that establishing what the text *meant* is a first step toward deciding what the text *means*. Exegesis, we might say, is the necessary preliminary to *exposition* (that is, saying what the text means to us today). Only so can we avoid the Scylla of antiquarianism and the Charybdis of eisegesis.

Understanding it then as a preliminary task for expositors, be they theologians or preachers, how should we do exegesis? First, let me insist on the necessity of exegesis for the preacher. One of the things I learnt just forty years ago in Germany at the Stift or Seminary (Lutheran) in Tübingen is that no sermon is truly a sermon (that is, a proclamation of the Word of God) unless it is based upon a sound exegesis of the text. This is because it is not the preacher's task to bring before the congregation his own opinions, whether on religion or any other matter. It is precisely to allow the Word of God (which as we saw in the last chapter is to be found exclusively in Scripture's witness to Jesus Christ) to speak to the congregation. Thus exegesis is a necessary preliminary task for the preacher. Without it what he says in the pulpit will not be authentic proclamation.

Most New Testament departments in Protestant seminaries in the United States circulate guidelines for exegesis for the use of their students, and the doing of an exegesis is often the major course requirement in biblical studies. In England it is more usual to comment on biblical passages ("gobbets"), which is rather different as it tends to atomize the text. Here is an outline of the method we use for our students in the Virginia Theological Seminary (Protestant Episcopal). We are constantly modifying and adapting it in the light of further experience, so it has no claim to be the final product. We also work in close cooperation with our department of homiletics.

The first thing to do is to make one's own initial paraphrase. Before consulting any other books, exegetes should read their pericope (that is, the passage prescribed by the day's lectionary, or in a nonliturgical tradition, a passage of their own choosing), with two questions in mind. First, what did the author say? And second, what did he mean? In answer to these questions write out your own initial paraphrase. Ideally, of course, you would do this using the Greek text, and if you can, so much the better. But most have to be content with an English version. People often ask me which is the best English version to use. The answer is, it depends on what you are trying to do. For this stage of exegesis, the best version is the most literal. For the less literal a translation is, the more you are dependent on the translator's opinions. It is you who have to make the interpretative decisions to the best of your ability, not leaving that to the translator(s). The most literal (and yet at the same time textually modern) translation is the Revised Version, or in the United States the American Standard Version, of 1881/1901. This is not always easily obtainable, however, and in this seminary we use instead the Revised Standard Version of 1952/1971 as our official text. This is not ideal, for while remaining pretty literal (like its predecessors AV and RV [KJV and ASV], on which it is based), it strays without warning into paraphrase, especially in the Epistles. How much should your own initial paraphrase vary from your most easily obtainable literal translation? Answer: At those points where your own preliminary understanding of the text leads you to express something in your own words rather than in the words of the translation.

You must not be too enamored of your initial paraphrase. Every further step in exegesis is intended to correct or modify it. If what you discover in these later steps simply confirms what you have proposed originally, you need not bother to record it. (I always have to insist that my students show up *only* what causes them to alter their initial paraphrase: theoretically they could show up a blank paper after that paraphrase, but that has never happened!) Record what deepens, extends, modifies, or corrects.

It is at this point that textual questions come up for consideration. You need to be sure that you are following what is most likely to be nearest to the original text. The vast number of textual variants are unimportant and do not affect the meaning. But occasionally they do. If you are using an English version rather than the Greek text, you will find that the principal textual variations are indicated in the marginal notes. Should you simply accept the decisions of the revisers? If you know nothing about the methods of textual criticism, you will have to. If you have Greek and are using the Bible Society's text, you will find much help in Bruce Metzger's *Textual Commentary*.[2] While on this subject, be careful, if you are using the Revised Standard Version, that it is an edition of 1971 or later. The earlier editions rejected readings which have since come to be generally accepted (for example, the longer text of the institution narrative at the Last Supper in Luke 22:19b–20). Unfortunately, the New English Bible still has the shorter text here, and this is just one example of the way this particular version falls short of the standards of contemporary textual criticism. It is as out of date here as it is when it gives the prices in shillings (which will soon perplex the English reader as much as it does the American).

You have now decided the precise text you will work upon. Your next stage is to make a list of the theologically significant words in your pericope. I mean really significant. Students often comment on relatively insignificant words. If for instance your pericope included Rom. 3:25 you would want to investigate the words "expiation," "blood," "righteousness" certainly. Possibly also "faith" and "divine forbearance," but in this verse you could certainly pass over "God" and "sins," as their meanings are fairly obvious here. You may find as a result of this step that you will want to change one or more words in your original paraphrase.

The fourth stage (assuming that you have done the text-critical stage; if not, the third) is to study the syntax of the passage, the way the words are put together. Look with care at such things as the tenses of the verbs, the structures of the sentences, the connections among phrases and clauses. If anything really significant leaps to your mind, record it, and use it when you come to make your final paraphrase. If nothing, then don't bother. It will help you at this stage, especially if you don't have the original languages, to compare a number of English translations. It is at this point that you reach for your NEB or JB, or even more paraphrastic versions such as Phillips. The next thing to look at is the *context* of the pericope. Keep in mind what you know as a whole about the book it comes from. How does this particular passage fit into the Gospel, Epistle, historical or prophetic book from which it is taken? Look at the immediate context, the pericope immediately before it and the one after it (unless of course it occurs at the end of a major section or book). Does the context affect or color its meaning? If so, how? Record the results of your investigation.

The sixth stage is to interpret the pericope historically. It is at this point that you will find it helpful to use a commentary. (Incidentally, it is not recommended that you invest in all the volumes of a given series. Find out which is the best commentary on a particular book.) Ask yourself these questions:

a. What was the *Sitz im Leben* (context in life, historical situation) of this book?
b. Was the writer using earlier tradition here? If so, did he significantly alter or modify that tradition in order to say what he wanted to say in his own particular situation?
c. How does this pericope fit into the overall situation in which the book in which it occurs was written?

Record the results of your investigation for your final paraphrase.

Now you should be ready to write a final paraphrase, revising your initial one where necessary in the light of your discoveries as you have conducted steps 2–6. This final paraphrase should say what you think the author meant and how his readers understood what he said. Remember, it has reference to the situation of the author and his readers, and does not necessarily say what it would mean today in your situation or that of your congregation. Before you can decide that, you have to engage in the next stage, that of exposition. Now here are some general considerations before we leave this subject.

Of all the various stages in exegesis, it is the historical situation that is the most important, in fact it is really more important than the question of authorship, as Willi Marxsen has observed.[3] It makes a difference for instance to the context in which you place a Pauline letter if you think it was written not by Paul himself but by a disciple of Paul after his death, because this changes the situation.

In doing his exegesis the preacher must not be frightened of critical positions. Even though he is not necessarily going to share his positions with his hearers, it will make a difference to his interpretation of a pericope. It is helpful, for example, to distinguish between the Letters Paul pretty certainly did write (the *homologoumena*, or generally acknowledged, as we call them nowadays) and those about which there are varying degrees of question (the *antilegomena*). This releases the latter (2 Thessalonians, Colossians, Ephesians, pastorals) to be treated as evidence for the subapostolic period and for "early Catholicism." By the latter we mean that phase in early Christianity when the excitement and expansion of the apostolic age gave way to institutional consolidation.

These considerations will be important for our exegetical work. By recognizing these writings as deutero-Pauline, we shall avoid making them more Pauline than they actually are or harmonizing them with the genuine Pauline teaching, and will allow them to have their own say.

In interpreting texts from the Gospels, it is most important that the preacher should not take them naively as straightforward reports of the historical Jesus. This is especially so when dealing with the Fourth Gospel, but it is becoming increasingly important for the synoptics, too. All four Gospels in fact contain three layers of tradition. The uppermost layer consists of the evangelist's own compositional work—what in the case of the synoptists we call the redaction. In the case of the Fourth Gospel we call it composition, as there the term redaction is generally used for the editorial touches which, as is commonly believed, were added by a later member of the Johannine school, the Johannine redactor. The redaction, or composition, expresses the theology of the evangelist. Underneath this topmost layer there is the pre-Gospel tradition. This consists of the sayings and memories of Jesus as they were creatively handled in oral transmission. In this stage they were shaped to serve the various activities of the early communities—preaching, catechesis, liturgy, apologetic, and polemics. The bottom layer consists of the authentic memories and sayings of the earthly Jesus during his ministry, beginning with his baptism and culminating in his crucifixion. Knowing at which level a particular tradition originated helps greatly in understanding its original meaning, and is therefore important in establishing what the text meant.

A knowledge of redaction-critical method becomes particularly important if the preacher is using the type of three-year lectionary introduced by the Roman Catholic Church in 1969, followed by the Lutheran, Episcopal, and other churches in the United States. This lectionary was commended by the bishops at Lambeth 1978, and it is a matter of great regret on the west side of the Atlantic that the Liturgical Commission of the Church of England has seen fit to propose a two-year lectionary of its own in common with the Free Churches. We feel that this is being very insular! In the three-year lectionary we have one year devoted (in the main) to Matthew, one to Mark/John, and one to Luke. Such an arrangement challenges the preacher to concentrate on the redactional level of the evangelist of each particular year. The same challenge would present itself if the preacher were following the old Reformed custom of working through one book at a time, if the book he was taking were one of the Gospels. An example of misunderstanding I came across after the three-year lectionary was introduced was a preacher's complaint that the same incident came up more than once a year, each time from a different Gospel. But the very repetition of the same incident challenges the preacher to pay particular attention to the specific evangelist's treatment of the incident.

Perhaps the worst, and most easily succumbed to, temptation is that of harmonizing. This means putting together information derived from more than one Gospel in order to reconstruct what the interpreter supposes to be a historical scene. I heard a notable example of this recently. For years, on the First Sunday in Lent we had the Matthean form of the temptation story. Now in the Mark year we have, naturally, the Marcan form of the temptation, which is much shorter and has a distinct character of its own. But instead of concentrating on this distinctive character, the preacher informed his congregation that Mark had not told us the full story of what had happened, and that to know this we had to go to Matthew or Luke—a leap which left him preaching on the three temptations exactly as in bygone years! If he did know the three temptations from the double tradition of Matthew and Luke, Mark obviously felt he could dispense with them and give the meaning he wanted to the temptation without them. The preacher should have followed suit, as he would have done if he had done a proper exegesis on his text.

The distinction between the three levels of gospel tradition provides a greater wealth of material for the preacher. A good example would be the parable of the sower. As originally told by Jesus, it would be the pure parable more or less as we have it in Mark 4:3–8. Later, the missionary church added the edifying allegorical interpretation, pointing out the dangers awaiting the new converts in the missionary churches. At the final stage the evangelist Mark inserted verses 10–13 between the parable and its interpretation. This emphasizes the mysterious character of the revelation brought by Jesus, a favorite interest of Mark's. The preacher would have to decide, in the course of his exegesis, which level of the tradition he wanted to use for his sermon. The greatest mistake, made by some who are introduced for the first time to historical-critical method, would be to dismiss as of no value anything that does not go back to the earthly Jesus. His Word is a living thing, which has to be applied anew in each situation—and thus the tradition accumulates.

Many of the Sunday Gospels are miracle stories. Again, it is helpful here to distinguish where possible between the three levels: Jesus, the tradition, and the redaction. As I have argued elsewhere,[4] there is a level of genuine historical memory in the miracle stories. We have sayings in which Jesus speaks about his exorcisms and healings, while the actual stories are based on a general memory that he performed such things as part of his ministry. For him they were actions which attested to the eruption of the Kingdom of God in his own presence, word, and work (see, for example, Matt. 12:28 par.; Matt. 11:2–6 par.). After Easter these memories were preserved and shaped into stories proclaiming Jesus as the prophet of the end time (for example, Luke 7:11–17) or as Son of God (for example, Mark 3:7–12).

Then we come to the redactional level of the miracle stories. Mark was faced by a situation in which some people were in his opinion laying so much stress on Jesus as a miracle worker that they soft-pedaled what really mattered, his suffering and death on the cross. Their version of the gospel was too triumphalist, as we might say today. Mark of course accepted the miracle tradition; he had no intention of denying that the miracles ever occurred. But he does try to tone them down and to set them in a wider perspective. Hence the messianic secret, which plays such a prominent role in Mark's redaction (cf. especially Mark 9:9). His miracles have to be kept secret until after the cross and resurrection. Only then will their true meaning become apparent. Only then will it be possible to make a true confession of Jesus as the Son of God. He is Son of God only because he is the suffering Son of man. The miracles thus became what Austin Farrer aptly called "prefigurations" of the supreme messianic miracle, Jesus' passion and resurrection. In this way redaction-critical method can be of great help in preparatory exegesis for a sermon. It is a Lutheran principle that every sermon should preach the cross. A redaction-critical exegesis of Mark's treatment of the miracles will enable the preacher to do just that.

The signs of the Fourth Gospel seem to have passed through a similar development. In the case of those which are unique to the Fourth Gospel, especially the Cana wine miracle, it is hard to be certain what the original tradition was, but clearly at some stage all these miracles have been used as simple proofs that Jesus was the Son of God, that is, the Messiah (see John 20:31). But by the time of the evangelist, this use of the miracles has proven inadequate. Mere miracle faith is not enough. So the evangelist transforms the miracles into launching pads for his great discourses. When Jesus feeds the multitude, he is thereby revealing himself as the bread that came down from heaven. When at Siloam he gives sight to the man born blind, he reveals himself as the light of the world. And when he raises Lazarus from the grave, he exhibits himself as the resurrection and the life. Theoretically, it might be legitimate for the preacher to treat the Johannine miracles as simple proofs of Jesus' divine sonship (as the earlier stage of John's Gospel did). But in this case it would seem to be more edifying to treat them as the evangelist himself treats them—as a revelation of who Jesus is.

Historical-critical exegesis will help the preacher when dealing with the passion narratives in Holy Week. Recent attempts to overturn the thesis of the older form critics such as Dibelius, who held that the passion narratives originated as continuous stories rather than as isolated units of tradition, need not be taken too seriously. There is ample evidence to suggest for instance that John's passion narrative is quite independent of Mark's, and there is much to suggest that Luke knew a non-Marcan continuous passion story, too. Given the fact that the early Christians were Jews, and that they would have continued to celebrate the Passover but in a Christian way, it is only natural to suppose that they would have shaped the passion story as a Christian Passover haggadah.

From what is common to the three passion traditions (Matthew/ Mark, Luke, and John) it is possible to reconstruct a primitive outline of events. Jesus was arrested by the Jewish authorities, subjected to a preliminary hearing, which resulted in a decision to accuse him before Pilate as a messianic pretender and therefore as a dangerous revolutionary. Pilate sentenced him as such and he was executed by crucifixion at the hand of the occupying power. But such a bare factual account never appears in the New Testament. Even our hypothetical pre-Gospel passion narrative already contained theological interpretation. For the earliest Christian preaching presented the death of Christ thus: "Christ (Messiah) died for our sins in accordance with the scriptures" (1 Cor. 15:3 RSV). Here are three theological assertions: First, Jesus died as Messiah, God's anointed One. The primitive Christian kerygma, or preaching, seized upon this undoubted fact and turned it around: it was precisely as God's Messiah that Jesus died. But that caused a major problem, for the unbelieving Jews certainly, and for the believers themselves very probably. How could God have allowed his Messiah to suffer the shameful death on the cross, to be placed under the curse for all who were hanged upon a tree (Deut. 21:23)? Answer: he died according to the scriptures. Here the reader will recall what was said earlier about the psalms, with their pattern of suffering and vindication, and the picture of the vicarious sufferer in Isaiah 53. Once they had seized upon that chapter, the early Christians were carried further in their theological understanding of Jesus' death. Not only was it in accordance with God's plan of salvation that he should die and be vindicated. It was positively the means of salvation: he died *for our sins.* He gave his life as a ransom for many (Mark 10:45, a verse which many scholars believe to be based upon Isa. 53:10–11).

Already the earliest passion narrative was shaped to proclaim these theological truths. *Jesus died as Messiah.* That is the topic of the investigation of Jesus by the Sanhedrin. Various groups dress him up and hail him ironically as claimant to the throne. Pilate condemns him as would-be King of the Jews. *He died according to the Scriptures.* Whether the Scriptures are cited as proof texts as in Matthew and John, and once in Luke, or whether they are allusively echoed as particularly in Mark, all the passion narratives are impregnated with the language of the Old Testament. *He died for our sins.* This has not colored much of the narrative, but it was developed particularly in the liturgy and therefore appears in the supper accounts of Mark, Matthew, and the longer text of Luke. In their preparatory exegetical work preachers will have discovered these theological motifs in the passion narrative. If they are to preach the passion, they cannot content themselves with the bare facts of the tradition. Nor is it biblical to paint the sufferings of Christ in lurid detail. They should also be very careful to avoid encouraging any anti-Semitic feeling which can be easily triggered off by talking about how the "Jews" crucified Jesus. Rightly understood, the Gospels offer no sanctions for either of these treatments. Rather, preachers must bring out these theological understandings of the passion: he died as Messiah, he died in fulfillment of God's promises and in accordance with the whole pattern of God's dealings with his people. And he died for our sins:

> He died that we might be forgiven,
>   He died to make us good;
> That we might go at last to heaven,
>   Saved by his precious blood.
> ("There Is a Green Hill Far Away"
>   Cecil F. Alexander)

But the evangelists have incorporated these traditional passion narratives into their Gospels, and by so doing each has given them a particular slant of his own. Mark, as we have seen, was concerned to portray Jesus not simply as a wonder worker but as the one whose miraculous healings prefigured the supreme miracle of the cross.

Jesus achieved that salvation for us by taking upon himself the fullest consequences of human sin although he himself was sinless. As St. Paul worded it, "For our sake he made him to be sin who knew no sin" (2 Cor. 5:21 RSV). St. Mark, by means of his narrative, makes the same point by the only words he allows Jesus to speak from the cross: "My God, my God, why hast thou forsaken me?" All the way through the passion narrative, Mark had highlighted the isolation of Jesus: betrayed by one disciple, forsaken by the rest, denied by Peter, jeered at by the Roman soldiery, the Sanhedrin, and the crowd, railed at by the two thieves by his side on the cross—then finally forsaken by his Father.

By and large, Matthew reproduces Mark's passion narrative, adding a few touches of his own here and there, of either apologetic or legendary character. (Matthew was in controversy with the Jews at Jamnia; hence, for example, the guard at the tomb to counter the charge that the disciples stole the body.) Luke apparently had an independent passion tradition of his own, which he supplemented by information from Mark (a not very fashionable view today in redaction-critical circles, but we still believe it). As Martin Dibelius put it, Luke transposed the passion from the key of tragedy to the key of pathos. He presents Jesus as the example for Christian martyrs—of whom there were probably a growing number by the time Luke wrote. John, on the other hand, presents Jesus in his passion as almost—to quote Käsemann's half-truth—like a God striding the earth. Jesus is master of the whole situation. He calls the shots. The temple police and the detachment of troops are paralyzed when they come to arrest him in the garden, and he has to urge them to do their duty: thus he sets the whole drama in motion. And so on all the way through until finally he dies, not with Mark's cry of dereliction, but with the triumphal shout "It is accomplished" (not "It is finished," as the RSV feebly, following KJV, translated it).

In Eastertide there will be a call for preaching on the postresurrection stories. I say postresurrection because actually there is in the New Testament no story of the resurrection itself. There is no description of how God raised Jesus from the dead, or of his egress from the tomb (we do get that in the apocryphal Gospel of Peter). For the resurrection, which by definition occurs precisely at the point where this age, the age of history, comes to an end, and where

God's new age beyond history begins, is inaccessible to the historian. All we have is the effects of the resurrection in history, like the craters left behind when a bomb explodes. These two craters are the empty tomb story and the appearance stories.

The empty tomb story is the earlier tradition, for Mark, our earliest Gospel, has only that. The main thrust of this story is the Easter proclamation, uttered by the young man, an angelic figure at the tomb: "He is not here, he is risen." For the rest, the interpreting figure points forward to appearance in Galilee, where Peter will be inaugurated as the foundation of the church and the disciples will be launched on their mission of proclaiming salvation through the Jesus event (cf. Mark 16:7 with 9:9). Mark probably had no appearance stories; he apparently knew only a list of appearances (16:7) like that we find in 1 Cor. 15:5–8.

In course of time appearance *stories* developed, and we find them in all three later Gospels. These are not historical narratives, but expressions of the meaning of the Easter experiences of the community. It is the Easter event that founds the Christian community and inaugurates its mission. It is the Easter event that makes the two Sacraments (Baptism and Eucharist) vehicles of the presence of the risen Lord. It is the Easter event which led to the experience of the Holy Spirit. John dates the giving of the Spirit by the risen Lord on Easter Day (John 20:22), while Acts places it on the day of Pentecost. The difference is merely one of theological accent.

In this attempt to illustrate how the historical-critical method can help the preacher to identify how Christ is preached in the New Testament, we have concentrated thus far on the Gospels. Something also needs to be said about the Epistles, a passage from which is provided by the lectionaries most Sundays as a possible preaching text.

The Epistles are addressed to those who have already accepted the apostolic preaching of Jesus as the saving act of God (see for instance 1 Thess. 1:5–10). They assume a knowledge of this preaching and expound its doctrinal and ethical implications, often in face of what the Apostle views as false teaching by his opponents. This is especially the case with Galatians and 2 Corinthians. The doctrinal parts of the Epistles are not a series of revealed propositions of a theological kind, nor flights of the apostle's speculative imagination.

Rather, they are attempts to draw out for teaching or polemical purposes the implications of the kerygma, the apostolic message of the saving event. A clear example of this is the way Paul deals with the problems raised by the Corinthians about the resurrection of the dead (1 Corinthians 15). Starting with a reminder of the kerygma as he originally delivered it, the Apostle proceeds to deduce its implications for the problem in hand. In the same way, the ethical parts of the Epistles (technically known as *paraenesis*) are not a series of catechetical imperatives dropped down as it were from heaven, nor ethical ideals thought out by the Apostle himself. Rather, they are illustrations drawn from traditional catechetical formulas of the life-style appropriate to those who have accepted the Apostle's message and entered the Christian community through Baptism. Preachers in their exegetical work would need to pinpoint the kerygma behind the doctrinal expositions and ethical exhortations.

Both the ecumenical three-year lectionary and the British two-year lectionary have restored the Old Testament reading. It has been a criticism of the three-year lectionary that with the exception of the Lenten season, which presents a series of highlights from Israel's salvation history, it always subordinates the Old Testament lesson to the liturgical Gospel and does not allow the Old Testament to speak in its own right. As a result such doctrines as creation, providence, wisdom, and even the demand for social justice tend to get short shrift. Instead, the relation of the Old Testament lesson to the day's Gospel encourages almost invariably a christological exegesis of the Old Testament text. That is to say, the lectionary offers those passages which, whether as type or as prophecy, can be interpreted as pointing forward to the Christ event. Now there is much to be said in favor of the christological interpretation of the Old Testament. In fact, Brevard Childs in his commentary on Exodus has broken new ground by offering a "canonical" exegesis, as he calls it. After seeking to establish the meaning of the text from its origin through oral tradition and earlier documents to its final redaction, Childs then adds a section in which he traces the way in which an Old Testament passage is interpreted christologically in the New Testament. He believes that we have not established the meaning of the text in the church until we have done that. We should often treat the Old

Testament that way, and in the British two-year lectionary there is a chance to do this when the Gospel or Epistle passage is the "controlling reading" of the day. But when in the two-year lectionary the Old Testament provides the controlling lection, then the preachers in their exegeses must allow the Old Testament to speak for itself, with its own theme.

NOTES

1. In an address to the Society for New Testament Studies meeting in Durham, North Carolina, in August 1976, Professor Robert Funk welcomed the shift of leadership in biblical studies in the United States from the great interdenominational seminaries (Union, Harvard, and Yale) to the departments of religion in the state universities where, free from ecclesiastical control, the New Testament could be studied together with other literature of antiquity in a humanistic context. Anyone who had experienced the shift in Europe in the thirties from theological liberalism to the revival of biblical theology could only register a déjà vu in reverse.

2. Bruce M. Metzger, ed., *A Textual Commentary on the Greek New Testament* (London and New York: United Bible Societies, 1972).

3. Willi Marxsen, *Introduction to the New Testament* (Oxford: Basil Blackwell; Philadelphia: Fortress Press, 1968), pp. 10–11.

4. Reginald H. Fuller, *Interpreting the Miracles* (London: SCM Press; Philadelphia: Westminster Press, 1963), pp. 18–45.

3

From Exegesis to Preaching

A few voices in the scholarly world today are questioning the adequacy of a purely historical-critical exegesis. Biblical texts do not come straight to the contemporary church from the original authors or from the communities which first received them. They come to us through centuries of use in the church. This concern is expressed in different ways. We have already mentioned how Brevard Childs believes that the exegete should go on to show how the text came to be understood in the New Testament. My former colleague, James A. Sanders, expresses a similar concern. Texts, he says, continue to have a life of their own in the believing community and acquire new meaning. As an Old Testament and intertestamental scholar he is thinking primarily of the Old Testament texts and the way they were understood in pre-Christian Judaism. But the same holds good of the New Testament texts. They come to the church today—including the preacher—through centuries of tradition. Now this sounds daunting. It suggests that before preachers can expound the text for today they have to study the exegeses of the church fathers, the schoolmen, the reformers, and the post-Reformation divines! Such study however is the task of New Testament scholars, and even they would only be able to scratch the surface.

Fortunately, the way the Bible comes to preachers is in the context of the liturgy. It comes to them—at least in the liturgical churches—in a lectionary where each pericope is related to other pericopes: an Old Testament reading, a New Testament reading (other than the Gospel), and a Gospel. As we have noted earlier, the pairing off of a particular Old Testament text with a particular Gospel pericope gives the Old Testament text a christological slant. When Isaiah 53 comes with the passion narrative, you are bound to treat it as a prophecy of

Christ's saving work on the cross. Again, the text comes on a particular day in the church year. It is remarkable how a text can speak differently on different occasions. For instance, in the traditional lectionary of the 1662 Book of Common Prayer and of the American Book of 1928, the feeding of the multitude occurred three times in the church year, twice in the Johannine version (Sunday next before Advent and Lent IV), and once in the synoptic version (Trinity VII). The Sunday before Advent highlighted the verse, "This is indeed the prophet who is to come into the world" (John 6:14 RSV). Lent IV by contrast would highlight the theme of refreshment. Jesus fed the multitude in the wilderness with as much as they needed; so he refreshes us with the sacrament as we pass through the wilderness of Lent. In the Trinity season the story speaks with an ethical accent: it challenges the church to concern itself with bread for the hungry. Preachers therefore should always keep an eye on the liturgical context of their pericopes and ask themselves, what does this text say in this particular service today? It will help to have a sound understanding of the rationale of the church year.

A second aspect of the liturgical context is that the text of a eucharistic lectionary is read and expounded to a congregation which is about to partake of the Holy Communion. How does the message of the pericope relate to this? If for instance the Gospel of the day is the healing of the paralytic, its message, "Your sins are forgiven you," is actualized when the people come up to Communion and receive in the Sacrament the remission of sins and all other benefits of Christ's passion. If however the principal service is Morning Prayer, this consideration will of course not apply—which only goes to show that such a service is a torso, to quote Karl Barth.

A third way in which the liturgy provides a framework for the interpretation of a text is that it is shortly followed by the recitation of the creed. All recent revisions of the liturgy have restored the order: readings, sermon, creed. (If the sermon is preached at the Daily Office of Morning or Evening Prayer, it is desirable that it should be preached after the lesson and before the Apostles' Creed, as the rubric of the new American prayer book suggests.) The creeds do not add anything to biblical faith, for as Article VIII says, they are to be accepted because they "may be proved [that is, tested] by most certain warrants of Holy Scripture." But they do highlight the central message of the Bible: creation; redemption through the incarnate life, death, and resurrection of Jesus Christ who is Lord and Son of God; the Holy Spirit; the church as holy, catholic, and apostolic; the second coming; and the hope of eternal life. Radical theologians disparage the creeds. They complain that the creeds say nothing about matters which are important for modern Christians, such as the Eucharist. But since the Nicene Creed is recited at the Eucharist anyway, that seems a mere quibble. Others have complained that they say nothing about social justice. But such concerns are expressed in other parts of the liturgy, for example, in some of the newer collects and in the prayers of the people. What I am pleading for is the use of the creeds as a hermeneutical framework for preachers' interpretation of the Bible. Their exposition of the biblical message should lead them to proclaim the great message of God as Creator, Redeemer, and Sanctifier. The creeds steer them to the central message of the Bible. In the last resort the creeds point them to Jesus Christ.

While preachers will often find help from the liturgical context in which the sermon is set, this will not do the whole job. There is a place for such liturgical preaching, but it is not the whole of preaching nor the only style. The congregation consists of individual persons who have brought with them their own hopes and fears, their attitudes and their aspirations, their personal problems and perplexities. Preachers as pastors will have become familiar with all these things by visiting their people at home, by meeting them in group sessions and in pastoral counseling, and maybe by hearing their confessions. Preachers may be able to identify a situation in their people's lives which is analogous to a situation to which the biblical text was addressed in its day. The task then is to readdress the biblical message away from its original hearers to the present congregation, just as when you forward a letter to a different address. Of course preachers need to be circumspect in preaching this kind of sermon. They would not want to unveil the private life of any member of their congregation to anyone else in the process! Rather, they would take some *typical* kind of contemporary personal situation, say a parent with teenage children on drugs, and describe it in such a way that their hearers can become involved and identify with it, and then bring the biblical message to bear upon the situation.

My colleague Milton Crum, professor of homiletics at Virginia Theological Seminary, suggests a threefold structure for all sermons:

1. Situation
2. Complication
3. Resolution[1]

There is something profoundly biblical about this structure. It is true to the Pauline antithesis of law and gospel: we are sinners (situation); the law convicts us of sin and exposes our need of redemption (complication); then comes the gospel message of salvation (resolution). I think this is an excellent way of addressing the scriptural text to the hearers if and when the pericope itself follows this pattern, if—to use the contemporary jargon—that is the story line. It is a particularly good model, for example, when the text is one of the parables of Jesus, like the great Lucan story parables—the good Samaritan or the prodigal son. Preachers can get their hearers to identify with one of the characters of the story and carry them along through the character's vicissitudes to the final solution. Some recent scholarly exegesis of the parables which pays particular attention to their literary structure and their story line will be very helpful here.[2]

But I question whether the threefold structure should be made the *invariable* pattern for the sermon. First, there is the practical question of producing boredom in one's hearers by constant repetition of the same structure. How will the congregation react if for fifty-two Sundays a year they are taken through the same threefold process? Secondly, one of the things I learned in Germany (this was directed against the popular division of the sermon into three parts like ancient Gaul) is that *the structure of the sermon should be determined by the structure of the pericope*. I am therefore inclined to say, by all means pattern your sermon according to the three stages of situation-complication-resolution when the pattern of the text itself demands it. But do not force that pattern on the text, and when it does not have the pattern, take the opportunity to follow a different structure.

This brings us to another related question. Ought our preaching to be "from above" or "from below"? By "from above" I mean starting with the biblical word from on high as conveyed through the text and then relating that word to some contemporary situation. Sermons "from below," on the other hand, start (as in Milton

Crum's threefold scheme) by constructing a human situation with which the congregation can identify and then bring the biblical word to bear upon it.

During the church struggle in Germany in the thirties, sermons "from above" were very much in vogue, and it was even a point of principle *not* to give any practical application! In theory this was to let the Word speak for itself; in practice this sprang from a cautious avoidance of getting involved in current politics—understandable when the Gestapo were present taking down notes of everything that was said. Of course at that time one could generally assume that everyone knew the situation and could make one's own application. Perhaps, too, this is a matter of national and ecclesiastical temperament. British and American congregations are most likely to get involved with the sermon if it starts with the people and then addresses the biblical word within that situation. They like to be engaged. German congregations on the other hand appear to have a higher appreciation for pure theology! In any case, preachers should be aware of what they are doing and occasionally vary their practice when the text seems to require it.

Thus far we have considered addressing the biblical text to personal situations. What about addressing it to social and political situations? During the sixties there was much talk about "worldly Christianity," the secular meaning of the gospel, about "letting the world set the agenda for the church." There was an impatience with purely religious and spiritual concerns. In many quarters the pendulum has swung the other way during the seventies. One now hears the demand that preachers confine themselves to spiritual matters and keep out of politics. Here again, the preacher ought to be guided by the text. This incidentally is one of the advantages of preaching from a lectionary. The text is given. Preachers do not decide to talk about politics, the text constrains them to do so. They are simply acting responsibly as ministers of the church which put the lectionary in their hands and said, "This is the Word of God to the church today." If the situation to which the text was addressed has its closest analogy in a current social or political situation (as will be the case particularly with the preexilic prophets or the Lucan parables), how can they preach on that text by avoiding politics or social questions? A text like the parable of the good Samaritan seems to leave no option to the preacher in an opulent suburban parish but to preach upon the current social and political problems created by affluence and poverty. The last occasion I preached on that parable I told a suburban congregation that they should not oppose a city income tax on commuters, not a popular message at the time. If the congregation realizes that the preacher is submitting responsibly to a given text, rather than constantly riding a personal hobby horse, they are more likely to hear the word of God, however unpalatable it may be.

Translating the biblical message from one culture into another is not an easy matter. Here the warnings of such radicals as Dennis Nineham are well taken. There *is* a great cultural chasm between the twentieth century and the first. Let us take one example. Suppose a preacher were dealing with that very difficult passage 1 Cor. 11:2–16, where Paul regulates the role of women in the church. He calls for women prophets to be veiled and justifies this partly by appealing to Genesis 1 and 2 to support the subordination of women. Does fidelity to Scripture demand that even if we do not enforce the practical ruling (veiling of women prophets), we should certainly teach the subordination doctrine? We know today that this doctrine was derived from contemporary culture, which Hellenistic Jews shared with Stoic philosophy. And we know that the scriptural basis Paul gives for it is an illegitimate extrapolation. For Paul combines Genesis 1 and 2 in a way that no exegete would do today, arguing that God created man (male) in his own image, but woman in the image of man, whereas Gen. 1:27 states quite clearly that God made both man and woman in his own image directly. Is there any Word in 1 Cor. 11:2–16 which speaks to the church today? The real concern of Paul in these chapters is to order Christian worship in such a way that it causes no offense or scandal to the outsider (see especially 1 Cor. 14:23). In those days women prophets speaking unveiled would have been cause for a scandal. Today nobody would take any notice of a woman speaking in church without a hat on! What then would cause scandal for the outside world? Surely it is that a community which professes that God made both man and woman in his own image, and that in Christ Jesus the difference between man and woman is transcended (Gal. 3:28), denies these basic truths of creation and redemption by excluding women from its priesthood. So in order to be true to Paul's intention in his text, it may sometimes be necessary to give a practical ruling which is the precise opposite to what he gave! It is absolutely necessary that we fasten upon the *intention* of a text, not the cultural *form* in which that intention is expressed. Then we must look at the contemporary situation and ask ourselves, how can we implement the intention of that text today?

As we survey the task of moving from exegesis to preaching, we observe that preachers are concerned with two poles—the text and the contemporary situation. It is their task to build a bridge between these poles. To do this they need to know as much as they can about both poles. Not only do they need to know the Bible, they need to know all they can about the contemporary world and its culture. It is not that this culture determines the Word which is to be spoken to it, for the Word comes from Scripture. But the contemporary culture will surely determine how the Word is to be spoken today, and how it is to be redirected. So along with constant study of the Scripture, the preacher should be au courant with what people are reading and thinking in the world. That, I take it, is what the exhortation in the old ordinal meant when it said at the ordination of a priest that he must "draw all his studies this way."

It is a daunting task. Who can be sufficient for these things? Who can dare to be minister *verbi divini?* We can only trust in God to make us able ministers of the new covenant.

NOTES

1. Milton Crum, *Manual on Preaching: A New Process on Sermon Development* (Valley Forge, Pa.: Judson Press, 1977).

2. See J. D. Crossan, *In Parables: The Challenge of the Historical Jesus* (New York: Harper & Row, Publishers, 1973).

4

Putting It into Practice

In this chapter we shall present first an exegesis done by the present author in a homiletics class at the Virginia Theological Seminary. This exegesis followed all the steps outlined earlier in chapter 2 and was done impromptu in response to a challenge from a member of the class. It is not the thoroughly scientific exegesis one would do in a graduate seminar in the New Testament but the kind of exegesis preachers might aim at doing in preparation for their sermons. It concludes with a synopsis of a homily constructed on Milton Crum's threefold pattern of situation, complication, and resolution. The text was taken from the Propers of Pentecost 5 Year A in *Services for Trial Use* (1971) of the Protestant Episcopal Church. Since then this book has been superseded and in the new *Book of Common Prayer* (1979) the text is appointed as Proper 7 (which may fall on one of the early Sundays of the post-Pentecost period, its exact liturgical date being determined by the date of Easter in the given year). Also, the text as now used begins at verse 24, and may optionally include verses 16–23.

This sample exegesis has been distributed to students in homiletics courses in the Virginia seminary for several years, and has even been pirated by an evangelical publishing house which had earlier placed some of my works in New Testament on their index of proscribed books!

TEXT: MATTHEW 10:26–33

1. *Initial paraphrase,* using a two-phase process.

   a. First, we seek to answer the question, What does the author say? with a *literal translation* from the Greek text, as follows.

(Non-Greek students can find literal translations in Alfred Marshall, *The R.S.V. Interlinear Greek-English New Testament,* and semiliteral translations in the "American Standard Edition" of the Revised Version, 1901.)

> Do not, therefore, fear them,
>> for there is nothing veiled
>>> which will not be revealed
>> and nothing hidden
>>> which will not be known.
> What I say to you in darkness
>> say in the light,
> and what you hear into the ear
>> proclaim upon the houses.
> And do not fear from the people killing the body
>> but being unable to kill the life; but
> fear rather the one able to destroy
>> both life and body in gehenna.
> Are not two sparrows sold for an *assarion,*
>> and one of them shall not fall upon the ground without your father.
> Now even the hairs of your head, all of them, are counted.
> Do not, therefore, fear.
> You are more valuable than many sparrows.
> Everyone, therefore, whoever shall confess in me
>> before human beings,
> I too will confess in him
>> before my father, the one in the heavens.
> And whoever shall deny me before human beings,
> I too will deny him
>> before my father, the one in the heavens.

Translation/meaning problems of *key words* were noted, to be addressed in step 2.

(1) V. 28. Meaning of *psuchē*? Does it mean "soul" or "life" or what?

(2) V. 29. Meaning of the phrase "without your father"? (This raises a theological question about the relation of God to events in history and exemplifies the interaction between one's theology and one's exegesis.)

(3) V. 32. Phrase *homologēsei en emoi,* "confess in me": is it to be taken literally?

b. The question, What does it mean? answered with the *initial paraphrase*.

> So don't be afraid of your persecutors.
> Everything which is obscured at the moment
>   will be brought to light later on.
> Everything which is concealed for now
>   will be known later.
> The teaching I am giving you in the secrecy of darkness
>   you must tell out in the daylight.
> And what you hear me whispering to you privately
>   proclaim publicly.
> Don't be afraid of those who put you to death physically,
>   but cannot destroy your real life(?)
>   and the physical life in gehenna.
> You can buy a couple of sparrows for a nickel,
>   but your father cares for them
>   even when they fall sick or dead on the ground (?).
> God even knows how many hairs you have on your head,
>   so don't keep on being afraid.
> You are much more precious to him than lots of sparrows.
> Consequently, those who confess me before people
>   I will confess before my heavenly father at the eschaton.
> Whoever denies me before people
>   I will deny in the same way before my heavenly father.

(Beware of becoming too enamored with the initial paraphrase. The question marks indicate its tentativeness.)

2. The *interpret lexically* step, exploring the meaning of key words. (Three words studied, namely, those noted in step 1 as exegetically significant.)

a. *Psuchē*: Using a Greek concordance (the only reference used), Matthew's use of the word was surveyed.

2:20. Those seeking the child's *psuchē* are dead.
6:25. Do not be anxious about your *psuchē*.
10:39. One finding his *psuchē* will lose it, and one losing his *psuchē* for the sake of me will find it.
11:29. You will find rest for your *psuchē*.
12:18. My *psuchē* is well pleased with my beloved.
20:28. The Son of man came to give his *psuchē*.
22:37. You shall love God with all your *psuchē*.
26:38. My *psuchē* is grieved to death.

In the above references, Matthew uses *psuchē* in some passages to refer to physical existence, as the "body" in the passage being exegeted. But in other passages, notably 10:39; 11:29; 12:18; 22:37; 26:38, as well as 10:28, the term seems to refer to the *perissoteron ti* of Luke's parallel, and this "something more" seems to indicate the fullness of relationship with God. Thus the substantive *psuchē* of Greek thought was rejected in favor of *psuchē* as an existential dimension of human life discerned in the immediate context.

So the translation becomes, "Do not be afraid of those [note the plural] who can put to death physically, but fear only the one [note the singular] who can destroy your relationship with God."

(In translating *psuchē* in this passage as "relationship with God," the seminar under my guidance made the awesome and risky leap which must be made for the Living Word, who spoke through the text to Matthew's readers then, to speak to us, Matthew's readers, now.)

b. The phrase "without your Father" was then paraphrased as "without a relationship with your Father," the evangel for the reader being that you have a relationship with God in which not a single aspect of your life, even your death, is outside his care, even when you are under persecution.

c. *homologeō*: Using the literal meaning of the word, we translated it "to say the same thing that God says." When your *word*, your total behavior before people, corresponds to the reality of God's relationship with you, the fact that you believe and trust this relationship is confirmed before God.

3. In the *interpret syntactically* step, we discern (a) a literary structure, (b) thematic content, and (c) theological affirmation in the passage.

a. From a *literary* point of view, the passage is a string of aphorisms:

v. 26,	initial aphorism
v. 27,	parallelism
v. 28,	complementary parallelism

v. 29,   parabolic application
v. 30,   parallel parabolic application
v. 31,   personal application
vv. 32–33, exhortation to fearless confession in the form of
            what Käsemann calls a "sentence of holy law."

b. *Themes* in the passage:

  (1) Do not be afraid. (There must have been a salient prob-
      lem of fear.)
  (2) Do not hide your relationship with God in Christ, for this
      reality will inevitably make itself known.
  (3) Do not be afraid of your persecutors, who can only de-
      stroy your physical body, because there is only one per-
      son who can destroy the caring relationship God has for
      you.
  (4) God's caring relationship with you is certified by his car-
      ing relationship with even the lowly sparrow. How much
      more with people!
  (5) The one thing that can destroy the caring relationship
      with God is your negating it by not behaving in cor-
      respondence with it. Therefore, you with your potential
      for lack of faith and trust are the only one to fear.

c. Theologically, the evangel, which the passage affirms, is
   God's care for his people, even now in the time of persecution. (See steps 4 and 5 for references to persecution.)

4. The *interpret contextually* step. An examination of (a) the
   Matthean context and (b) the synoptic context.

   a. Regarding the Matthean context, we conclude that the pas-
      sage is part of Jesus' charge to the Twelve as they prepare
      to go out on mission and that it is part of the second of
      Matthew's five "Great Discourses." The passage begins with
      "therefore," which connects it with the previous talk about
      persecution.

   b. Examining the synoptic context, we find the following:

      In the Lucan version (12:2–9), we find
      (1) no use of *psuchē*, but use of the suggestive "anything
          more";
      (2) an additional phrase, "Yes, I tell you, fear him";

(3) *five* sparrows sold for *two assarions*;

(4) the "Son of man" confesses before angels of God, in contrast to Matthew's "heavenly Father," which is a favorite phrase for Matthew; and

(5) the Lucan phrase "I say to you," which is probably more true to an original "Amen, I say to you."

The most significant exegetical clue found in the synoptic survey is Luke's suggestion in his "anything more" that he would interpret *psuchē* as a dimension of human life beyond mere physical existence—possibly a dimension so vast that he cannot name it but only point toward it. (Using Luke as a clue for interpreting Matthew is an application of the hermeneutical principle of using Scripture to interpret Scripture.)

5. In the *interpret historically* step, we conclude:

Concentrating, in this case, on the Matthean setting in the primitive church, Matthew is writing in and to a church faced with persecution by the continuing adherents of the synagogue. Matthew's audience would be in this *Sitz im Leben*, so he is writing to encourage them to confess Jesus openly, even though such a confession would mean expulsion from the synagogue and its corollary social ostracism. (Note that the pastoral-theological concern of Matthew is being discerned. Later, as we move to the meaning-for-him stage in the process, we will seek an analogous here-and-now *Sitz im Leben*.)

6. The final stage is a *summary interpretation* which includes (a) an understanding of what objectively the text said and meant to its first readers, and (b) an understanding of what the text means to the person who is exegeting it.

a. Our understanding of what objectively the text said and meant to its first readers, in the form of a final paraphrase:

You need not be afraid of the persecution
    which faces you in relation to the synagogues.
Whether you are kicked out or not
    is not "the be-all and the end-all" of your life,
    for the way things really are with God
    will be known openly no matter what.

What I have told you privately
   tell other people openly.
And do not be afraid
   of those who can put you to death physically
   but cannot destroy your relationship with God.
Rather, be afraid of the one (namely yourself)
   who can destroy both your physical life
     and your relationship with God
     as if thrown into the trash dump of gehenna.
Don't you know
   that even though sparrows sell two for a penny
   not one of them falls to the ground
   outside a caring relationship with your Father?
But with you,
   even the hairs of your head are numbered by him.
Therefore,
   don't be afraid;
   you are worth more than many sparrows.
So everyone
   who declares by open behavior
   his or her relationship with me,
   I will declare that relationship before my Father
     (thus confirming your actual relationship with God as
     demonstrated by your behavior).
But whoever denies caring relationship with me,
   I will deny before my Father
     (thus confirming your actual negative relationship with
     God as demonstrated by your behavior).

(We have experienced the exegesis of a passage addressed to people who were fearful of demonstrating their relationship to God in Christ, faced, as they were, with persecution. The theological root of this fear seemed to be that they were valuing physical, social, and economic life at the expense of their relationship with the caring God in heaven. So the caring relationship God has for us is proclaimed with vivid imagery to enable the reader to live boldly and demonstratively for and by his faith reality.

The objective understanding having been stated, the next step is to state the meaning for the exegete, which meaning is shared in preaching. With sensitivity for the concrete situation of the passage's original *Sitz im Leben* and for its pastoral-theological concerns and for its evangel, the structure and content of a sermon are incipient in the exegesis, especially in the final paraphrase. In the exegesis, the exegete tried to be true to the text, and in so doing the text became true for the exegete and through him for the class. This truth is summarized in step 6b, which follows.)

b. Our understanding of what the text meant to us in the form of the synopsis of a homily, which was later shared with the class.

Situation	Like the Christians to whom Matthew wrote, we are sometimes so afraid of opposition and criticism by other people that we do not demonstrate, by living out and declaring, our relationship with God in Christ, so we strain or destroy our relationship with him; and
Complication	this fear of opposition issues from thinking that our social and economic relationship with other people and our physical life are ''the be-all and the end-all'' of existence; but
Resolution	Jesus witnesses to a caring relationship with God our Father through him, a relationship which nothing, not other people, not physical death, nothing except ourselves, can destroy, and in the strength of this relationship with our Father, we are less afraid of human opposition or even death.

FINAL NOTE: This exegesis was done in one two-hour class period. Drawing on my knowledge eliminated taking time for reference to lexicons, word studies, dictionaries, or commentaries. Yet this exegesis demonstrates a procedure which conscientiously wrestles with the text and which any preacher-exegete can practice in a reasonable length of time.

In the rest of the examples given in this chapter I shall not offer a complete exegesis. Instead, I shall seek to determine after preliminary discussion of the pericope (a) the original situation of the scriptural author and his readers or addressees; (b) what the original author was saying to that situation, and how it would have been understood by the original audience or readers. After that I shall proceed to identify a contemporary situation such as the preacher might be confronted with, and indicate how he might change the address of the message so that it says the same thing today to the contemporary situation as it said in the original one. The passages selected are taken from the two-year lectionary printed at the back of the Church of England *An Order for Holy Communion,* Series III (1973).

Year 1: Advent 3

Isaiah 40:1–11
1 Corinthians 4:1–5
John 1:19–27

First Lesson: Isaiah 40:1–11

This is the opening passage of the work of Deutero-Isaiah, or the unknown prophet of the Exile (Isaiah 40—55). In ca. 540 B.C. the victories of Cyrus of Persia over the Babylonians are shortly going to make possible the return of the exiles from Babylon to their homeland in Palestine. The unknown prophet hears a "voice"—not a voice in the wilderness, as the New Testament citations of this text have it, but the voice of a member of the heavenly council, where God and his angels are deliberating about what is shortly to happen. Verses 1–2 speak of the impending return, while in verses 6–8 the prophet is commissioned to proclaim the triumphant purpose of God. In verses 9–11 the prophet is further commissioned to address those who are still at home in Zion and Jerusalem, who had not shared the experience of the Exile. They are told their compatriots are about to come home, and to pass on the message to other cities in Judah.

This passage is often classed as a prophetic call (cf. Isaiah 6 and Jeremiah 1), and the message he is entrusted with in these verses is a succinct summary of the message of Deutero-Isaiah as a whole.

Second Lesson: 1 Corinthians 4:1–5

Much of Paul's correspondence with the Corinthians is taken up with a defense of his apostolic authority against criticism in the community at Corinth, either internal criticism as here or, as was the case later on, by interlopers from the outside.

We don't know exactly what charges the Corinthians were leveling at Paul—and his colleagues, as the plural indicates—but from the way he defends himself we can infer that they judged him by certain criteria which were inapplicable to the apostolic ministry. Apostles and their colleagues are, Paul insists, ministers of Christ and stewards of the mysteries of God. That is to say, by their ministry the apostles and their colleagues exist to incorporate believers into the Christian salvation history or the paschal mystery, and to foster their growth in it. Consequently, the thing to look for from the apostles is that they be faithful to that commission, not to whatever other standard the Corinthians were judging them by. Paul notes that his own conscience is clear, but conscience is not a final judge—the final judge is the Lord, and his judgment will be pronounced at the last day. However, neither Paul's own clear conscience nor the accolades he receives (if he gets any) from other people are any guarantee that he is really being faithful to his commission. Only the Lord will pass final judgment on his ministry, and that at the last day.

Gospel: John 1:19–27

Verse 19 provides a title to this pericope: "The testimony (or witness) of John the Baptist" (henceforth JBap). This testimony is given in response to two interrogations. The first is a negative testimony: JBap says what he is not: not the Christ (that is, Messiah, v. 20), not Elijah (v. 21), not *the* (that is, the expected) prophet like Moses in Deut. 18:15. All he is is a voice, like that spoken of in Isaiah 40 (we have seen how that verse has been utilized in the New Testament), preparing the way of the Lord in the wilderness. Then comes the second interrogation: why does John baptize, if he is not the Christ, Elijah, or the prophet? Answer: his baptism is merely a preparatory baptism for the Coming One. (The next section goes on to narrate John's identification of the Coming One with Jesus, and his sending his disciples to join Jesus.)

The Gospel of John operates on two levels. First, there is the historical level. JBap really did baptize, and he interpreted his baptism as preparatory for the advent of a Coming One (he did not know it was Jesus: see Matt. 11:3). JBap never made any messianic claim for himself. It is highly probable that he used Isa. 40:1 about himself as the people of Qumran did about themselves. But there is another level to the Gospel. The evangelist (or the Johannine tradition at an earlier stage) is faced with the problem of "continuing baptists," that is, those who continued to follow JBap and made messianic claims for him. So he represents JBap as uttering an explicit denial to any possible messianic claim, a perfectly correct interpretation of JBap's attitude. (His renunciation of the claim to be Elijah stands in formal contradiction to the purported recognition of JBap as Elijah by Jesus in Mark 9:12–13: the contradiction however is not real. It is a difference between two different conceptions of Elijah. In Mark 9 Elijah is a forerunner; in John 1 Elijah is himself a messianic figure. Both Jesus' statement in Mark and that of JBap in John are theological interpretations, but interpretations of two differently circumstanced communities.)

Homily

In the season of the year between Advent 1 and Pentecost, the situation of the congregation is most obviously a liturgical one. On the Third Sunday in Advent it is preparing to celebrate Christmas. These readings are chosen to that end. (In fact, they are all traditional Advent readings from earlier lectionaries.)

First, let us take the Gospel in conjunction with the Old Testament reading. In this case the link is Isa. 40:3/John 1:23: a voice crying in the wilderness, make straight the way of the Lord. This involves a reinterpretation of Isaiah (see above), but we must take it as the Gospel takes it, for this is where the Isaiah text comes finally to rest. The impending event proclaimed today is no longer the return from exile but that of which the return from exile is a type, namely the Christ event. JBap was the herald who prepared Christ's advent, and we listen to him preparing us today for the Christmas celebration.

It is a little odd when you come to think of it that JBap has gone down in Christian lore as the herald of Christ's advent. For surely Christ had already come (in his birth) when JBap appeared in the wilderness. His voice is not heard until Jesus is a full-grown man and about to embark on his public ministry. But that's just the point. The advent of Christ, the event which the season of Advent prepares for, is not just his birth at Bethlehem but his *coming in its totality*, the Christ event as such.

Now there are two basic ways of proclaiming the Christ event. Either it can be expressed (as is more normal) in paschal terms: Christ died and was raised again. Or we might say, in advent-epiphany terms, the sending of the Son of God into the world, or his coming into the world. Christmas celebrates the mystery of Christ in this way. And the figure of JBap, who is central to this Sunday, points to this understanding of the mystery. If the preacher takes the Old Testament reading and the Gospel together, his message should be the proclamation of Christ's total coming, which will be celebrated in the Christmas festival.

But there is another possibility. This is suggested by taking the Gospel together with the Epistle reading. The Epistle reading speaks about the Apostle and his colleagues. But what Paul says there is permanently applicable to the Christian ministry. (Remember this is the beginning of Ember Week in Advent, and ordinations will be coming up shortly; perhaps there will be an ordination in the preacher's own church, though unlike American bishops, who often ordain in local parishes—a wonderful experience—English bishops unfortunately usually ordain in their cathedrals only.) Whether an ordination is coming up locally or not, the relation between pastor and people is a perennial concern in any congregation. There is a link between Paul's portrait of a Christian pastor as a minister of Christ and steward of the mysteries of God and JBap's self-portrait as not Christ, not Elijah, not the prophet, but a voice, pointing away from himself to the Coming One. The preacher will perhaps recall Karl Barth's fondness for the Isenheim altarpiece by Matthias Grünewald. There we see JBap (quite unhistorically, but theologically suggestively) pointing to Christ hanging on the cross. That is what it means to be a minister of Christ and steward of the mysteries of God. We preach not ourselves but Christ crucified. So an alternative for the preacher today would be to expound the concept of the ordained ministry of Word and Sacraments as it emerges from the Epistle and Gospel so that the people will know what according to Scripture they have a right to expect from their pastor, and by what criteria they should evaluate his ministry.

Having discussed a sample series of readings for the Advent-Christmas-Epiphany cycle, we will now offer one sample from the paschal cycle, which runs from Ash Wednesday through Pentecost Sunday. We choose the following.

Year 1: Easter 3
Isaiah 61:1–3
1 Corinthians 15:1–11
John 21:1–14

First Lesson: Isaiah 61:1–3

This passage comes from Trito-Isaiah, whose prophecies continued the message of Deutero-Isaiah *after* the exiles had returned from Babylon to the Holy Land. The passage stands out from its context and functions as a prophetic call story, though it is told as a report rather than directly narrated.

The return from exile has proved a disappointment. There are still people among the returnees who are afflicted, the *anawim* or poor. These are the people the prophet is sent to encourage. He promises them that better times are on the way.

The canonical history of this text does not stop here, for Luke represents Jesus as making this the text of his inaugural sermon at Nazareth (Luke 4:16–30). There our passage sets out the program of Jesus' earthly ministry. He will proclaim the good news of the Kingdom and will conduct a ministry of healing as sign of the coming of that Kingdom. Given the use of Isa. 61:1–3 in the New Testament, it would have been more appropriate to include this reading in the Advent-Epiphany cycle rather than in the Easter season. For its Christology is that of the sending of the incarnate One into the world rather than of the death-resurrection-exaltation, which is the theme of the season for which it is appointed. For this reason, we shall find it more appropriate to connect this passage with the Church's mission (see below).

Second Lesson: 1 Corinthians 15:1–11

In the latter part of 1 Corinthians Paul is responding to issues and questions raised by the Corinthians, partly in a letter they have written to him (1 Cor. 7:1) and partly in the supplementary information brought along from Corinth to where Paul is, in Ephesus, by three members of the Corinthian community (Stephanas, Fortunatus, and Achaicus; 1 Cor. 16:17). Our excerpt is evidently dealing with a question raised in the supplementary information. The Corinthians deny that there is a resurrection of the dead (v. 12). They find such a notion incredible, absurd, and probably unnecessary to Christian faith. The traditional interpretation of this denial is that the Corinthians believed in the immortality of the soul in Greek fashion rather than in the resurrection of the body. More recent scholarship has offered an alternative, and to my mind more plausible, interpretation of the Corinthian position. Note that Paul never says they do not believe in the resurrection of the body. What he does say is that they could not accept resurrection *from the dead*. Their position looks like a gnosticizing one. They believed that when they came to Christian faith they had acquired a knowledge of heavenly realities, and through this knowledge they believed themselves to be already raised from the dead and therefore not requiring any further resurrection. This was the same sort of belief as that of Hymenaeus and Philetus in 2 Timothy 2:18. In other words, they held to an overrealized eschatology. Paul is going on to insist that only Christ has been raised from the dead thus far: other resurrections will not take place until his parousia (v. 23). All others will have to wait for their resurrections. Their present situation is characterized by a "not yet."

To provide a firm foundation for his ensuing argument, Paul first reminds the Corinthians of the gospel as he first delivered it to them in ca. A.D. 50 (he writes 1 Corinthians about five years later). He summarizes the gospel message in a creedal formula which he says he had received from others who were Christians before him. It is a recital of the central events of the paschal message, namely the death, burial, and resurrection of the Messiah for our salvation. The formula concludes with a list of resurrection appearances. Since these include two appearances to persons Paul names, Cephas (Peter) and James (the brother of the Lord), and since Paul met these two men on his fortnight's visit to Jerusalem in about 35 (Gal. 1:18), this tradition is almost firsthand testimony of eyewitnesses, given to Paul within about five years after the appearances had happened. We could hardly expect better evidence than that! Moreover, Paul includes his own apostolic call among these appearances (Acts 9, 22, and 26 view Paul's Damascus road encounter rather differently; there it is merely a visionary experience). Since Paul lists his apostolic call among the appearances, we may conclude that all the resurrection appearances were appearances of the risen and ascended Lord from heaven, not appearances of the resurrected but not yet ascended Lord as Luke-Acts suggests. The appearances had a dual purpose: to establish the Christian community and to inaugurate its mission. It is as an accredited witness, with the same testimony as his predecessors among the apostles (v. 11), that Paul can interpret the meaning of the resurrection from the dead for his Corinthian converts.

Gospel: John 21:1–14

Chapter 21 of St. John's Gospel is widely recognized today to be a postscript or epilogue to the body of the Gospel, added perhaps by an editor who was a member of what we nowadays refer to as the Johannine school. His additions throughout the Gospel have a more ecclesiastical thrust than the main part of the work. This chapter is concerned with the relative authority of Peter (whose primacy among the other apostles is universally recognized in the New Testament) and the Beloved Disciple, the founder and hero of the Johannine community (vv. 15–23). The story of the miraculous draft of fishes now serves as a setting for the latter discussion and, as the chapter now stands, is really incomplete without it, for resurrection appearance stories normally culminate in a word of commissioning from the risen Lord. It is probable that such a word of commissioning to Peter and to the others generally concluded vv. 1–14, perhaps a saying like "Henceforth you will be catching men" (so Luke 5:10 at the conclusion of a similar episode, but there located in the earthly ministry). The 153 symbolize the universality of the apostolic mission. The original conclusion will then have been lopped off to make room for the commission to Peter to feed the flock. The earlier form of the story was more evangelistic, the later form is more pastoral in its orientation. The earlier form was therefore an expansion of the traditions recorded by Paul in the Epistle reading: "He appeared to Cephas, then to the Twelve."

Homily

The connecting link between these three passages is the theme of commissioning for mission. In the Old Testament reading, Trito-Isaiah is called to deliver the message of liberation to the returned exiles, a passage which is picked up by St. Luke to describe the mission of the earthly Jesus. The tradition cited by Paul in the Epistle reading lists the postresurrectional appearances which inaugurated the apostolic mission, while the Gospel reading was originally a narrative of the first two appearances in Paul's list.

The change of the postresurrectional appearances to Peter and the other disciples from an evangelistic to a pastoral model is a reminder that while the reality of the church's mission is an abiding one, the form of the mission varies from time to time and from place to place. Peter Hebblethwaite, in his book on the three Popes of 1978,[1] tells us that at the Synod of Roman Catholic bishops in 1974 Cardinal Wojtila (now Pope John Paul II) noted how evangelization meant different things in different parts of the world. In Africa it meant facing the challenge of indigenization—not importing Western secondary baggage along with the gospel but producing a genuine African expression of Christianity. In Asia the challenge was how the gospel should be related to the non-Christian religions. In Latin America the challenge to the church was to identify with the poor and dispossessed (liberation theology, whose basic ideas spring from our Isaiah text). In Western Europe and North America the challenge took the form of secularism, and in the countries of the Communist bloc the form of atheism. To this last one might add, as the Pope himself made abundantly clear on his visit to his native Poland in the spring of 1979, the question of human rights. The Easter event then inaugurates mission. The question is, what form must the mission of the church take in our particular time and place? Today's text provides preachers with an opportunity to address this question for their own congregations. For mission is an integral aspect of the Easter message.

Year 1: Trinity 5

Exodus 24:3–11 (1–18)
Colossians 3:12–17
Luke 15:11–32

First Lesson: Exodus 24:3–11

The shorter version of this reading is very awkward. The longer reading is a combination of two variant accounts of the ratification of of the Sinaitic covenant, the one sandwiched into the other. The first is vv. 1–2, 9–18 (J version), the second vv. 3–8 (E version). Hence it would have been preferable for the shorter version to have only vv. 3–8 (E version). Adding on vv. 9–11, just part of the J version, is useless.

Here are the salient differences between the two accounts:

J VERSION	E VERSION
On the mountain.	Below the mountain.
Book of covenant.	Decalogue on stone.
Moses sole recipient; priestly representatives and elders have preliminary vision.	Moses mediates ratification: all the people participate in a single ceremony.
Ratification by sacrificial communion meal for representatives only.	Ratification by sprinkling of blood on altar (symbolizing Yahweh) and people.

Verses 3–8 were far more important in the ongoing tradition. The story is alluded to in later prophecy (Zech. 9:11), is taken up in the developed Marcan form of the cup-word at the Last Supper, and plays a prominent role in Hebrews, being cited at Heb. 9:20–22 and alluded to in Heb. 10:29. Sprinkling is also mentioned in connection with blood (that is, the sacrificial death of Christ) in Heb. 12:22–24 and 1 Pet. 1:2.

Thus the E covenant ceremony contributed importantly to the development in the early church of the doctrines of the atonement and of the Eucharist. The ceremony performed by Moses is a type of Christ's sacrificial death on the cross, which effects atonement and inaugurates the new covenant, and whose effects are constantly made available for our participation in the sacrament of the Holy Communion.

Second Lesson: Colossians 3:12–17

Colossians is one of the disputed letters of Paul. If it is not by him (and there are strong though not insuperable arguments against its Pauline authorship), it is by a member of the Pauline school, and the church rightly receives it as an expression of Pauline teaching. The normal pattern of a Pauline letter is to deal first with doctrinal and then with ethical questions. Our pericope is from the ethical part and therefore consists of "paraenesis," that is, ethical exhortation.

Form-critical analysis of the Pauline paraenesis has shown that this material belongs to an early Christian catechesis.[2] The opening exhortation, "Put on," recalls the putting on of the baptismal robe as the candidate came up out of the water. Such a connection of thought has probably been made already in Jewish proselyte baptism, from which the early Christian gentile mission seems to have borrowed much of its baptismal and catechetical practice. Then follows a list of virtues (Hellenistic Judaism took over such lists from the Stoics, and thereby discovered a new way of teaching the Torah to converts). But the teaching has been Christianized. As always in the Pauline paraenesis the imperative arises out of the indicative: Forgive one another; as the Lord has forgiven you, so also must you forgive. Agape appears as the unifying principle behind the specific virtues, a sentiment echoed by the Collect of Quinquagesima Sunday in the Book of Common Prayer of 1662 (American 1928; Proposed Prayer Book 1976, Epiphany 7): "charity, the very bond of peace and of all virtues." From verse 16 on, the pericope shifts from daily life to the community gathered for worship. It speaks of the ministry of the Word and the response to the Word in psalms and hymns and spirit-filled songs (v. 16). This verse suggests the important role of church music in liturgy, second only to the ministry of the Word and integral to it as a response. The concluding verse gathers up all of these injunctions as they cover both liturgy and life, the gathered community in the sanctuary and the dispersed community in the world, the church of Sunday and the church of Monday through Saturday. All life is to be conducted in the name of Jesus and all life is to be eucharistic (v. 17).

Gospel: Luke 15:11–32

Whenever the preacher is confronted with one of the Gospel parables, he is well advised to read up what Joachim Jeremias has to say about it.[3] Jeremias is not necessarily to be followed in his interpretations of the parables, which Norman Perrin has described as the expression of "a rather conservative Lutheran piety."[4] But for the religious and social and linguistic background of first-century Palestine Jeremias is superb, and such knowledge will often lead the preacher to the message of the parable and help him to drive it home to his congregation.

The first thing to grasp is that the prodigal son is a real human story and to be appreciated as such. The father is a real father, the sons real sons—not just ciphers for God and for two different types of human beings. This is indicated by the wayward son's decision, "I will arise and go to my father and say, 'Father, I have sinned against heaven and before thee.'" There is heaven—that is God— and there is the earthly father; they are quite distinct. (The use of this verse as one of the penitential sentences at the beginning of the daily office in the Anglican prayer books has tended to obscure this.) A particular point of value that Jeremias brings out is that when the father goes to welcome his returning son he actually runs—a very undignified thing to do for an elderly oriental. The son's carefully rehearsed speech is cut off midway: the father treats him as an honored guest. Then there is the elder son. He comes along and hears the noise of merrymaking and naturally wants to know what it's all about. When he finds out, he is very angry—an anger expressed by his words. He doesn't call his father "Abba"—no polite address at the beginning. He refers to his brother as "your son"— not "my brother." He contemptuously calls him "this fellow." But the father replies in affectionate tones: "Child," he says, "you jolly well ought to be glad your brother is home again."

What is the point of this parable? (Although his work is open to some criticism, the view of Jülicher that every parable has one point only is still generally accepted.) Jeremias thinks this is one of the double-edged parables, with the point in the second part, the behavior of the elder son. That point, for Jeremias, is that the parable is vindication of the good news in reply to its critics—the opponents of Jesus who have criticized his conduct in eating with the riffraff, the tax collectors and prostitutes. It is really the parable of the Father's love.

The trouble with this interpretation is that it depends upon the context in which the evangelist has placed it, not on the parable considered on its own, which is how it was handed down in the pre-Gospel oral tradition. The Lucan context is provided by Luke 15:1, "Now the tax collectors and sinners were all drawing near to hear him" (RSV). Further, Luke joins the prodigal son to the twin parables of the lost sheep and the lost coin, giving all three of them a similar function as a reply to the criticism of the religious authorities. Crossan however has sought to interpret the parable on its own, as Jesus first told it. As we follow the story line we become involved with and identify successively with the younger and the elder son. The parable is not loaded on either side. Each part carries equal weight. It ends with the wastrel indoors feasting and the stay-at-home son, the good guy, outside pouting. It is therefore, at the Jesus level, a parable of reversal. In identifying with the reversed fate of the two characters we experience the coming of the Kingdom of God and its power to reverse all our previous values. Taken like that, the parable becomes after all (though Crossan being a Roman Catholic does not see it) a proclamation of the Pauline-Reformation message of justification by faith only apart from the works of the law (Article XI—the preacher should always keep his eye on the Articles when doing his exegesis), that great reversal of all our natural pre-conceptions. Here is the gospel in the Gospel.

This also answers a question raised by Eduard Schweizer and others about the prodigal son. Older commentators used to find in it a much simpler gospel than the Pauline-Reformation gospel, namely that God forgives without the need of any atonement effected on the cross by his Son. But the real point is that the parable is a comment on what is happening in Jesus' word and work: the kingdom is coming, and all conventional human values are being reversed. The parable therefore implies both a Christology and a soteriology or doctrine of the atonement. For the activity of Jesus in his word and work, which is the coming of the Kingdom, culminated in his death on the cross. It is the whole activity of Jesus that justifies the ungodly.

Homily

Today's readings are a classical illustration of two points made earlier, namely the interpretative slant that is given to Scripture by its combination with other Scriptures, and its use on a particular liturgical occasion. Coming as I do from several years of experience of the new Roman Catholic lectionary, and having worked on the committee which adapted it for the use of the Protestant Episcopal Church, I recognized immediately that for us these readings would have been appointed for a Sunday in Lent. In that season, the Old Testament lesson in the Roman lectionary provides a synopsis of the highlights of Israel's salvation history, the Epistle often features Pauline baptismal catechesis, and the Gospel (if it is not one of the Johannine signs) material from the earthly ministry of Jesus in which the saving act of the cross is foreshadowed. So I immediately ask, what are these readings doing here, on the Fifth Sunday after Trinity, a season of the year when our primary emphasis should be on the living of the Christian life and on growth in sanctification? How is the preacher to handle these texts today? The answer I think lies in taking the Epistle reading as the controlling reading for the others, and within the Epistle, the central verse, 13, "As the Lord has forgiven you, so you also must forgive." Christian exhortation is never mere announcement of the law. It is always rooted in the gospel. Ethics are rooted in theology, they are always a response to what God has done. Behind the imperative there is always an indicative. The gospel, the theology, the indicative are given in the message of the atonement, exhibited in type in the ratifying of the covenant of Sinai, in which the people were sprinkled with the blood; fulfilled in the blood of Christ (N.B.: "blood theology"—to which Percy Dearmer was so allergic that he cut out all references to it in *Songs of Praise*—is integral to the Christian message), his sacrificial death upon the cross which is the forgiveness of the sinner. This message is implicit in the parable of the two sons and is succinctly alluded to in the central affirmation of the Epistle reading, "as the Lord has forgiven you." The preacher will not need to concentrate today on the doctrine of the atonement, for he will presumably have done this in Lent and Passiontide. But he should briefly recall it to his hearers, reminding them that they have come today in today's Eucharist to be sprinkled anew with that blood, and to point them to the response of agape in daily life and in liturgy. We can select either one or the other. If we select the area of daily life, we can depict forgiveness as the quintessence of agape, the unifying principle behind all virtues.

The last of Queen Victoria's Conservative prime ministers, Lord Salisbury, used to say (in an age when wistful agnostics claimed to retain the Christian ethic while abandoning its theology) that Christian ethics are really much harder to accept than Christian theology. Of no part of the Christian ethic is this so true as the imperative of forgiveness. Forgiveness is in the most literal sense supernatural, for it is high above what we as natural men and women are inclined to do. It is something that only those who are motivated by the experience of God's forgiveness through the atoning death of Christ have a hope of achieving.

If, however, the preacher chooses to concentrate on the response to the saving act of God in Christ in the context of liturgy, as suggested by Col. 3:16, he has an opportunity to speak of church music as an integral part of the church's life. I am afraid that in Anglicanism church music often takes a lower place in our priorities—in sorry contrast with Lutheranism. Among the Lutherans a *said* service is unknown, and not only hymns but the liturgy itself is almost invariably sung by the congregation, whether it be the daily office or the principal Sunday service. In our tradition the minister has the ultimate responsibility for the choice of hymns, and yet how few have any notion of what is appropriate to the season, to the point in the liturgy where the hymn is used, and to the Scriptures. Hymns are an important part of the impact of the Sciptures and the sermon. Today's Epistle reading therefore provides an opportunity to bring the Scripture to bear upon the whole subject of the parish's response to the gospel in the area of church music.

INTRODUCING FUTURE ESCHATOLOGY

Both of the new lectionaries, the Roman-Catholic-ecumenical and the Church of England two-year lectionary, agree in introducing the note of future eschatology toward the end of the post-Pentecost season, running into Advent 1. Since these lessons play a more prominent role than they did in the traditional lectionary (see however BCP 1662 Advent II and Epiphany VI, the latter a set of propers which in some years were used as the end of the post-Trinity period), and since they create problems for many preachers, it seems advisable to include a sample from them.

Year 2: Trinity 26, Second Sunday before Advent
Exodus 6:2–8 (–13)
Hebrews 11:17–29
Mark 13:5–13

First Lesson: Exodus 6:2–8 (–13)

This section is from the P tradition (the later, priestly account of Israel's foundation myth). It gives a slightly different version of God's first appearance to Moses from the primary call passage in Exodus 3. God reveals himself as the God of Abraham, Isaac, and Jacob (these figures provide the link with the past), and for the first time under the name of Yahweh. He promises to bring the people out of Egypt and to lead them into the promised land. The difference in the P version is the emphasis on God's covenantal call to Israel to be his people: "I will take you for my people and I will be your God." Since the earlier version of the call of Moses (Exodus 3) is used on this same Sunday in Year 1, it would seem reasonable to concentrate this year on this aspect of the story. The people of God is founded by an act of election (in Abraham, Isaac, and Jacob), of deliverance (through Moses), and with a promise of the land. They are pilgrim people being pulled toward a future goal.

This sets the pattern of salvation history in the New Testament. There, too, God establishes a new people by his acts of election and deliverance and with the promise of his final kingdom. It is the picture of the people "between the times," between Egypt and the Eretz Israel and between the first and second comings of the Christ. Each community experiences the "pull of the future."

Second Lesson: Hebrews 11:17–29

This passage, from the well-known roll call of the heroes of faith, covers the period of the patriarchs (vv. 17–22), and Moses (vv. 23–29), that is, the periods we have characterized as election (the patriarchs) and deliverance (Moses). It thus picks up and expands on the material in the Old Testament reading. It also carries the period of deliverance to the point where the children of Israel have crossed the Red Sea and are waiting to enter the promised land (the forty years in the wilderness are skipped over, and in the very next verse the walls of Jericho fall, the first act of the occupation of the land). This forms a dramatic conclusion to the lesson. The people are all poised for the conquest of Canaan and the occupation of the land, but it has not yet taken place. When God acts, his actions always contain the promise of more to come, and they leave us with a sense of "not yet," of incompleteness. The same is true in the New Testament, as we shall see.

Gospel: Mark 13:5–13

Today's reading is part of what is commonly called the Little Apocalypse (sometimes also the Synoptic Apocalypse). These verses deal with the events of history leading up to the end, that is, the parousia or coming of the Son of man. Our passage deals specifically with the warnings of false religious teachers who come with the claim "I AM." Then there are wars, earthquakes, and famines. Usually there is a fourth item, pestilence, but its absence here must be accidental. Then comes the charge to the Christian community to preach the gospel, followed by the prediction of persecutions and family strife. In the middle of the persecutions there comes the promise of the divine assistance of the Holy Spirit in the hour of trial (v. 11).

Two major problems arise in connection with this material. First, how much of it goes back to Jesus himself? Most modern scholars (a notable exception is G. R. Beasley-Murray)[5] would find it impossible to take this as an actual discourse delivered by Jesus in this form. The reason is that it seems contrary to what he says elsewhere, especially in the apocalyptic sayings in Q (preserved separately in Luke 17 and fused by Matthew with the Marcan apocalypse in Matthew 24). There Jesus says that the end will be sudden and unpredictable (see especially the sayings in Luke 17:24–37). The Little Apocalypse, on the other hand, represents Jesus as giving a series of signs leading to the end in such a way that its coming would be neither sudden nor unpredictable. The more likely view is that we have here material from three different stages in the tradition: (1) authentic Jesus sayings, (2) revivals of Old Testament sayings and the sayings of Christian prophets which have gained circulation during the pre-Gospel period, and (3) redactional additions by the evangelist. It is not too certain into which of these three classes any given saying should fall, and the views of commentators vary. We may be more certain about the redactional additions than of the other levels. These Marcan insertions would include the following:

But the end is not yet (end of v. 7).
This is but the beginning of sufferings (end of v. 8).
And the gospel must first be preached to all nations (v. 10).
But he who endures to the end will be saved (v. 13).

From this it is clear that Mark is concerned to dampen down premature excitement about the nearness of the end. This fits a situation around the fall of Jerusalem (A.D. 70).

The second major problem concerns the interpretation of apocalyptic material. This applies not only to Mark 13 but to all apocalypses and especially to the Book of Revelation. I have just experienced an example of this problem. In the same week that these words are being written a lady called me up on the phone. She was very concerned that none of the clergy she knew were telling their people the true meaning of the Book of Revelation. She saw in this book a precise prediction of what was happening in the world in July 1979—the decision of OPEC to raise oil prices, the consequent threat to the whole Western economy, the lack of leadership in the White House, etc., etc.! I had to tell her that I could not understand Revelation in this way. For me, a New Testament critic, it can only be understood as having been compiled by the writer with direct reference to what was happening and to what was about to happen *in his own day*. He thought that the crisis he was going through was the last great crisis of history, ushering in the end. And of course he was mistaken. History has continued since. What then is the preacher to do with such texts? He will perhaps sympathize with the Jewish New Testament scholar, Claude Montefiore, when he said that the Little Apocalypse is of very slight interest and of little or no religious value today. Such a conclusion however would be a sign of impatience. We may recognize that the discourse at least in its present form is not authentic to Jesus, that the author was thinking only of events in his own day, not ours, and that he turned out to be mistaken. Yet at the same time we may appreciate that along the way the author was granted insights into human history which are as valid for us today as when they were first uttered. Such insights would include the following:

1. History is in God's hands. He always keeps the initiative. (In this way we may agree with our fundamentalist lady that present world events are a judgment upon Western civilization but without believing that these events are predicted in the New Testament.)

2. History is an ongoing struggle between the powers of good and evil. In the struggle, as it proclaims the gospel, the church of Jesus Christ will often be called upon to suffer. It happened like

that under National Socialism in the thirties, and it happened quite recently in Uganda.

3. The final goal of history is not the evolution of a perfect society (the illusion of Marxism, which ignores the prevalence of original sin among the proletariat just as among the capitalists) but can only come from outside (the coming of the Son of man).

4. Tyranny always contains the seeds of its own destruction. God will judge all tyrants in the end, as he judged Hitler and Idi Amin.

Homily

The first two readings depict the church as a pilgrim society *in via*. The preacher has the opportunity to use these texts to shed light on that pilgrimage today. We are always on the march between the times between Easter and the parousia. We are not yet there, but we have glimpses of the promised land which enable us to endure to the end.

The Little Apocalypse material should not be treated as prediction of what is happening in the world at the present juncture of history, but it can be treated as a disclosure—insights into the meaning of all history, and therefore also into the meaning of that tract of history we are in today.

NOTES

1. Peter Hebblethwaite, *The Year of the Three Popes* (London, Cleveland, and New York: William Collins, 1979), p. 178.

2. Philip Carrington, *The Primitive Christian Catechism* (London and New York: Cambridge University Press, 1940), pp. 34ff.

3. Joachim Jeremias, *The Parables of Jesus,* rev. ed. (New York: Charles Scribner's Sons, 1971; London: SCM Press, 1972).

4. Norman Perrin, *Jesus and the Language of the Kingdom* (London: SCM Press; Philadelphia: Fortress Press, 1976), p. 106.

5. G. R. Beasley-Murray, *A Commentary on Mark Thirteen* (London: Macmillan & Co.; New York: St. Martin's Press, 1957).

Conclusion

The material in the first three chapters was tried out at a summer school for clergy, mainly Presbyterian, at the Union Theological Seminary of Virginia in Richmond, Virginia, in July 1979. Two questions were raised there which are of great importance and reflect a widespread concern amongst preachers.

The first question was, how can busy parish ministers or priests find time within their busy schedules to work through all the procedures of exegesis as laid down in the earlier chapters of this book week by week? The other question was, how much of biblical criticism should we share with our people from the pulpit?

In answer to the first question, one of the participants made a very valuable suggestion. This was that new ministers or priests are rather like surgeons at the beginning of their careers. They feel awkward; they have constantly to refer to the books, and the procedures take a long time. Gradually, however, surgeons acquire a facility and dexterity, together with a store of knowledge from previous experiences, which enable them to perform an operation in far less time than they needed when they were fresh at the job. It is like this with exegesis. Take word study for instance. When the major theological words have been studied, it will not be necessary to repeat an in-depth study when such a word comes up in a fresh pericope. Preachers will also already have read the standard introductions and will be familiar with the accepted *Sitz im Leben* of the various New Testament writings, and therefore they will not necessarily have to repeat that stage of exegesis except to refresh their memories. Since (if they are using the three-year ecumenical lectionary) each year takes a particular Gospel, they will have studied the *Sitz im Leben* of that Gospel in Advent and will not have to do so again for every

Sunday the rest of the year. When the year of that Gospel returns in the three-year cycle, they will first want to keep their eyes open to see if there has been any major shift in scholarly views about the *Sitz im Leben* of the Gospel. For this reason it is an advantage to subscribe to a journal which features reviews of exegetical works (see also the bibliography). Otherwise, they can refresh their minds from the notes they took three years earlier. They will have the same advantage with the Epistles, which in the three-year lectionary are used in course during the Sundays of ordinary time (that is, Sundays after Epiphany and Pentecost). The same applies to the use of Acts and Revelation during the Easter season. I am afraid I cannot offer this advantage to those who are using the old-tradition eucharistic lectionary or the British two-year lectionary, which proceeds thematically rather than book by book. If the worst comes to the worst, preachers should resolve to do a thorough exegesis in preparation for their sermons once a month as a minimum.

The second question is difficult to answer in a general way. How much one should communicate the results of biblical criticism to one's congregation will all depend on the circumstances. One principle however can be laid down. This is that the pulpit is not the time and place to teach biblical criticism as such, either in its methods or in its results. In fact, teaching of whatever kind is out of place in the pulpit. This goes equally for those who say they like to preach what they call "teaching sermons." Years ago, when I wrote my first book on the use of the Bible in preaching, *What is Liturgical Preaching?* (published in 1957 but long since out of print), I drew, following the current theology of the time, a sharp distinction between evangelistic preaching, pastoral preaching, and teaching (corresponding to *kerygma*, *paraklesis*, and *didache* in Greek). The place for evangelistic preaching is in a parish mission, the place for pastoral preaching Sunday by Sunday in the pulpit, and the place for teaching proper in the lay class. In my 1957 book the model I worked with was that of proclamation—announcing anew to a congregation, which has already heard it before, the gospel message. I would still adhere primarily to that understanding of preaching, although many authorities on preaching today like to operate with a somewhat different model, that of the story. The Christian gospel, as they see it, is God's story, and the purpose of preaching is to engage a person in the story so that he or she appropriates it at the personal level. It is also the story of the community. I do not see that these two models of preaching are really incompatible, since storytelling can be a mode of proclamation, but in any case they rule out teaching as the primary purpose of preaching. A teaching sermon so called is simply not a sermon, but something else.

The place for teaching, then, whether it be doctrinal, ethical, or biblical and critical, is in the lay class. Any teaching that occurs in the sermon is essentially a by-product. It may occur there, but it does not have to. It is not the primary purpose of preaching. How does this affect points of historical criticism? Sometimes it may be helpful to introduce a point of biblical criticism in the pulpit, but only if it assists in the proclamation of the gospel (or on the newer model, if it engages people better in the story).

When Rudolf Bultmann launched his program of demythologizing in the 1940s, he was concerned to remove what he regarded as the inauthentic *skandala,* or stumbling blocks (which for him lay in the mythological language in which the kerygma was couched), in order that people might be exposed to the authentic *skandalon* of the cross. Sometimes the preacher's pericope may contain an inauthentic *skandalon*, a stumbling block to faith, which can be removed by historical criticism. An example of such a *skandalon* might be (although whether it would actually be would depend a great deal on one's congregation) the subordinationist texts in the Pauline Epistles ("Wives, obey your husbands"). Biblical criticism tells us that the household codes, in which this subordinationist ethic occurs, originate in Stoicism, whence they were adapted by Hellenistic Jews of the diaspora for instructing proselytes to Judaism from the Hellenistic world. Their purpose was to incorporate the best ethical teaching of the day into the Torah. In the New Testament, Christian teachers adapted these household codes in turn from Hellenistic Judaism and gave them a slightly Christian veneer by saying that wives have to obey their husbands "in the Lord." Thus the early Christians were not seeking to restructure a nonpatriarchal society but to transform a patriarchal society from within. Applying this teaching to today, the church would not be obeying these texts if it sought to restore the patriarchal society which these texts take for granted, for it is not the patriarchal society as such which presents the demand of God, but rather its transformation through Christianization. Accordingly, the preacher may well be helping to remove the inauthentic *skandalon* (if his congregation lives in a Western society in which there is equality between the sexes) and at the same time exposing the real thrust of the text, which is the Christianization of the given social structures of the day. Here, biblical criticism might really help to remove an inauthentic *skandalon*.

Now let us take another example which is more difficult. In the Fourth Gospel Jesus says, "Before Abraham was, I am." Taught by the modern criticism of the Fourth Gospel, the preacher will know that this is not an "authentic" saying of Jesus. That is to say, Jesus never uttered such a statement about himself. Criticism tells us that it is a saying which probably began as an utterance of Wisdom about herself in the wisdom tradition of Judaism. Jesus is here presented as a spokesman, and even more, the incarnation of the heavenly wisdom. This is like the Matthean saying, "Come to me, all who labor and are heavy laden, and I will give you rest" (Matt. 11:28 RSV). Here again, as we see clearly from Ecclus. 51:23–27, Jesus is being presented in these texts as the spokesman of the heavenly wisdom. Will it help or hinder the congregation if the preacher says that this is Johannine (or Matthean) theology, rather than an authentic saying of Jesus? It will depend upon the general attitude of the congregation. If they have already been exposed to modern critical method they may find it a relief to be told that the earthly Jesus never actually said that. For the Johannine saying may cause them an offense because for them it would contradict what they have come to appreciate as the truly human character of our Lord. On the other hand, to tell that to a congregation totally ignorant and perhaps strongly opposed to the critical method might put a real stumbling block in the road to faith. Of course there is a true message in the saying, "Before Abraham was, I am." To begin with, this saying is rooted in the claim of the historical Jesus to speak for God. He appears in the authentic traditions in the synoptic Gospels as one who dares to speak and act for God. But God did not begin to speak or act for the first time in the ministry of Jesus. God had been speaking and acting ever since the creation of the world and particularly in Israel's sacred history. He is a God who has not been perceived for the first time in Jesus, a wholly strange God, but a God who is recognized as the God they knew before, incarnated in Jesus. How will the preacher get his people to have this kind of an encounter with God? By telling them that while everything Jesus said and did he says and does from God's side, and that although he never actually said, "Before Abraham was, I am," this saying does truly capture what the ministry of Jesus had going for it? Or by ignoring the critical problem, and treating it naively as an authentic saying of Jesus? It will depend on which way the preacher can best communicate the meaning of the saying to his people, how best he can lead them to encounter with a God in Jesus who revealed himself already in creation, providence, and history. In the pulpit what matters is getting the message across, and whichever route—facing up to the critical problem squarely or ignoring it—will do that is the best way for the preacher to proceed. All the same, though, I should have preferred to do the critical spadework first in the context of an adult class, rather than in the pulpit. With a congregation which has had that preparation I would probably say in the pulpit, "As the Christ of the Fourth Gospel says, 'Before Abraham was, I am.'" I then don't have to compromise my critical integrity.

In speaking to laity in a classroom situation I have often been surprised how critical insights have come to them as a real liberation. I remember more than once speaking about the ascension story. I have carefully explained that in the earlier tradition the resurrection and ascension were regarded as a single indivisible event, and that the postresurrection appearances were regarded as appearances of the already resurrected and ascended Lord. And I have usually explained that I first learned this not from some wild-eyed, radical German critic but rather from an impeccably orthodox theologian, Bishop Michael Ramsey, from his early book *The Resurrection of Christ* (1945). So, far from this knowledge providing a *skandalon* to faith, people have welcomed it as a real relief. "I'm glad we don't have to believe in a literal ascension forty days after the resurrection, but why didn't the rector tell us that?" is the reaction I have met more than once. Candor however compels me to say that just recently I have had a very different reaction. This was from a Ugandan student, brought up by very conservative missionaries from England. He answered by producing his Bible and solemnly reading the ascension story in Acts 1, pointing out, "The angel actually did say

Jesus had ascended into heaven, and the disciples were looking up at him as he want to heaven. You are denying what the Bible says.'' It was useless in his case explaining about the biblical device of an *angelus interpres* (the device that is used also in the annunciation and birth stories and at the empty tomb to give the theological meaning of the event). For this student this had proved an authentic *skandalon*. It could only be removed by a lot of patient teaching, but I wondered if it was the right thing to transplant him from his culture to expose him to ours, and then send him back to Uganda again.

We might say, biblical criticism is for us preachers rather what the Jewish ceremonial law was for St. Paul. He was prepared to be all things to all people, if by any means he might save some (1 Cor. 9:20–23). To the Jews he was a Jew, to the Greeks a Greek, to those under the law as under the law, and to those free from the law free from the law himself. Should not the preacher similarly be prepared to become a biblical conservative to biblical conservatives if that is the only way they can hear the gospel? And then as a critic among those who have been exposed and who have accepted biblical criticism? If we find that inconsistent with our integrity, then we can only say that St. Paul, while he valued his personal integrity, was prepared to sacrifice even that so that Christ might be known, that in any case his gospel might be heard. Is this perhaps what he meant when he said of the apostolic ministers that they were ''deceivers, and yet true'' (2 Cor. 6:8)?

A Bibliography for Biblical Preaching

1. Basic Tools

For those with Greek:

The Greek New Testament. London and New York: United Bible Societies, 3rd ed. 1975. This text supersedes all other critical texts. The same text is printed in the Nestlé-Aland text which was published in the fall of 1979.

Thayer, J. H. *Greek-English Lexicon of the New Testament*, 4th ed. Edinburgh: T. & T. Clarke, 1930. Still useful despite its age, especially on the OT-Hebrew background of Greek words.

Kittel, Gerhard and Friedrich, Gerhard. *Theological Dictionary of the New Testament*. 9 vols. ET by G. W. Bromiley. Grand Rapids: Eerdmans Publishing Co., 1964–76. Requires some knowledge of Greek and Hebrew. It has taken over forty years to produce, and theological shifts have led to differences between earlier and later articles. Users should read the critique of the Wörterbuch method in James Barr, *The Semantics of Biblical Language*, Oxford: University Press, 1961.

Brown, Colin, ed. *The New International Dictionary of New Testament Theology*. 3 vols. Grand Rapids: Zondervan Publishing House, 1967–71. Also based on a German original, but extensively revised and expanded in a conservative evangelical direction. *Can* be used without knowledge of Hebrew and Greek, since words in these languages are transliterated.

For those without Greek:

The preacher without Greek needs first a very literal translation. The most literal version of the Bible based on a critical text is the Revised Version (American Standard Version) of 1881. The Revised Standard Version lapses occasionally into paraphrase. In addition to a literal translation other more paraphrastic translations should be consulted, for example, New English Bible, Jerusalem Bible, New American Bible, New International Version.

Richardson, Alan, ed. *A Theological Word Book of the New Testament*. London: SCM Press, 1950 and repr. Getting rather old now, but drew on the earliest articles in "Kittel."

2. Introductions

Anderson, G. W. *A Critical Introduction to the Old Testament*. London: Gerald Duckworth & Co., 1959 and repr.

Fuller, Reginald H. *A Critical Introduction to the New Testament*. London: Gerald Duckworth & Co., 1966 and repr.

Proclamation Commentaries, published by Fortress Press, consist of introductions to individual books of the Old and New Testaments used in course in the three-year lectionary.

3. General Works on Preaching

Wingren, Gustav. *The Living Word: A Theological Study of Preaching and the Church*. Philadelphia: Muhlenberg Press, 1960.

Bass, George M. *The Renewal of Liturgical Preaching*. Minneapolis: Augsburg Publishing House, 1967. A Lutheran scholar relates biblical preaching to the church year. Unfortunately his work antedates the new lectionaries.

Crum, Milton, Jr. *Manual on Preaching*. Valley Forge, Pa.: Judson Press, 1977. Combines a soundly biblical theology with literary and psychological insights.

4. Aids to Preaching

a. On the two-year British lectionary:

Cuming, Geoffrey, ed. *The Ministry of the Word: A Handbook to the 1978 Lectionary*. London: Bible Reading Fellowship, 1979.

b. On the three-year ecumenical lectionary:

Fuller, Reginald H. *Preaching the New Lectionary*. Collegeville, Minn.: Liturgical Press, 1973. Based on the original Roman Catholic form of the lectionary.

Proclamation 1 and 2: Aids for Interpreting the Lessons of the Church Year. Philadelphia: Fortress Press. Commentary and homiletical suggestions for all readings of the ecumenical lectionary, noting the variations between the versions of the various U.S. churches. The present writer has contributed the commentary for *Holy Week* (Series B) in Proclamation 1 and both commentary and homiletical aids for *Advent-Christmas* (Series C) in Proclamation 2.

c. Yearbooks of simple commentary:

Duckworth, Robin, ed. *This Is the Word of the Lord*. London: Bible Reading Fellowship; Oxford and New York: Oxford University Press, from 1980.

5. Listening to Sermons

Thompson, W. D. *A Listener's Guide to Preaching*. Nashville: Abingdon Press, 1966.

Howe, Reuel L. *Partners in Preaching: Clergy and Laity in Dialogue*. New York: Seabury Press, 1967.

6. Hermeneutics

Achtemeier, Paul. *An Introduction to the New Hermeneutic*. Philadelphia: Westminster Press, 1969.

Wink, Walter. *The Bible in Human Transformation: Toward a New Paradigm for Biblical Study*. Philadelphia: Fortress Press, 1973. His diagnosis of the bankruptcy of purely historical criticism reflects a widely felt concern. His proposed remedy (psychological) will command less assent.

Article "Hermeneutics" in *Interpreters' Dictionary of the Bible*.

7. The Authority of the Bible

Barr, James. *The Bible in the Modern World*. London: SCM Press, 1973.

Nineham, D. E. *The Use and Abuse of the Bible*. London: Macmillan & Co., New York: Barnes & Noble, 1976. These works are critical of the biblical theology approach, and Nineham particularly is radical in his attitude to the authority of the Bible.

Rogers, Jack B. "A Third Alternative: Scripture, Tradition and Interpretation in the Theology of G. C. Berkouwer," in W. Ward Gasque and William S. Lasor, *Scripture, Tradition and Interpretation*. E. F. Harrison Festschr.; Grand Rapids, Mich.: Eerdmans Publishing Co., 1978. A former fundamentalist seeks to establish a middle way between fundamentalism and radicalism, finding the inspiration and authority of the Bible in its witness to Christ.

8. Commentaries

a. Every preacher should possess at least one one-volume commentary on the Bible. The best are:

Peake's Commentary on the Bible. Ed. Matthew Black and H. H. Rowley. London: Thomas Nelson & Sons, 1952. This is mainly by British Protestant scholars.

The Jerome Biblical Commentary. Ed. Raymond E. Brown, S.S., Joseph A. Fitzmyer, S.J., and Roland E. Murphy, O. Carm. Englewood Cliffs, N.J.: Prentice-Hall, 1968. Known as the "Catholic Peake," this work is by American Roman Catholic scholars and thoroughly critical in its approach.

Preachers often ask what is the best commentary series to invest in. It is unwise to invest in a single series, as some volumes are always less good than others. The wisest thing is to buy the best commentary on each book. In the U.S.A. seminaries usually provide updated lists of commentaries on specific books of the bible for their alumni/ae.

b. For preaching in the latter part of Advent and at Christmas:

Raymond E. Brown. *The Birth of the Messiah: A Commentary on the Infancy Narratives of Matthew and Luke.* Garden City, N.Y.: Doubleday & Co., 1977. A superb piece of scholarship.

c. On the parables:

Jeremias, Joachim. *The Parables of Jesus,* rev. ed. New York: Charles Scribner's Sons, 1971; London: SCM Press, 1972. Highly informative on the Palestinian background of the parables. Seeks to recover their original form as told by Jesus and to relate them to Jesus' overall message. If the preacher decides to handle the parables at the Jesus level, this book is indispensable.

Crossan, John Dominic. *In Parables.* New York: Harper & Row, Publishers, 1973. By the analysis of literary structures Crossan helps the preacher to handle the parables (at the Jesus level) as story and to engage his hearers in that story.

d. We need a thorough treatment of all the parables at the redactional level. At the moment we have:

Kingsbury, Jack. *The Parables of Jesus in Matthew 13.* Richmond, Va.: John Knox Press, 1969.

Carlston, Charles E. *The Parables of the Triple Tradition.* Philadelphia: Fortress Press, 1975.

See also Schweizer, Eduard. "From the New Testament Text to the Sermon." *Review and Expositor* 72 (1975): 181–88. Schweizer expounds the parable of the sower (Mark 4:1–20) at all three levels (Jesus, the oral tradition, and the Marcan redaction) and demonstrates how this parable can be preached at any of the three levels.

e. The miracles of Jesus:

Fuller, Reginald H. *Interpreting the Miracles.* London: SCM Press, 1963. Expounds the miracle tradition in the Gospels at all three levels and offers suggestions for preaching the miracle stories.

f. Preaching on the passion:

It is important to understand the redactional treatment of the passion and to realize that in preaching, for example, on the so-called seven last words one is handling redactional theology rather than a tape recording of what Jesus said. To that end one should understand the way each evangelist presents the passion. See:

Evans, Christopher F. *Explorations in Theology* 2. London: SCM Press, 1977. Part 1, "The Passion of Christ."

g. Preaching on the resurrection:

Fuller, Reginald H. *The Formation of the Resurrection Narratives*. 1971.
   Reprint. London: SPCK; Philadelphia: Fortress Press, 1980. Contains
   homiletical aids.